GETTING THINGS DONE IN BUSINESS

Getting Things Done in Business

EDITED BY

EDWARD C. BURSK

EDITOR OF THE *Harvard Business Review* AND
MEMBER OF THE FACULTY, HARVARD GRADUATE
SCHOOL OF BUSINESS ADMINISTRATION

CAMBRIDGE, MASSACHUSETTS
HARVARD UNIVERSITY PRESS
1953

Distributed in Great Britain by
GEOFFREY CUMBERLEGE
OXFORD UNIVERSITY PRESS
LONDON

Library of Congress Catalog Card Number 52-12255
Printed in the United States of America

PREFACE

This book is based on the proceedings of the Twenty-Second National Business Conference, sponsored by the Harvard Business School Association, June 7, 1952, which was attended by some 1,200 businessmen — alumni and friends of the School — from all over the country and abroad.

The general theme of the Conference was "Getting People to Do Things." The morning session, consisting of five speeches developing the broad implications of the subject, is covered in Part I. The afternoon session, consisting of five panels dealing with specific problems in the same area, is covered in Part II.

The afternoon panels were conducted purposely on a very informal basis, in an attempt to let the subject develop as the group desired. Short talks by the panel members, aimed primarily at establishing their individual positions within the general subject area, were followed by a question and answer period. The discussion which ensued was dynamic and spontaneous; often it seemed to express the participants' inner convictions rather than the usual trite generalizations, and altogether it took up the major portion of the afternoon. As far as possible, this material has been reorganized into an orderly, consistent form, and fitted into the chapter-sections representing the observations of the various panel members.

Needless to say, the views expressed in any chapter or chapter-section are the responsibility of the individual author identified in the note at the beginning of the chapter, and as such are not necessarily representative of other authors or of the Harvard Business School Association.

I want to thank Miss Jane E. Hinchcliffe and Miss Virginia B. Fales for their very able editorial assistance.

September 8, 1952 Edward C. Bursk

CONTENTS

PART I

GETTING PEOPLE TO DO THINGS

Jervis J. Babb

As long as life has existed individuals and groups have been trying to get other individuals and groups to do certain things and act in certain ways. Admittedly, all these efforts have not been good ones. Nevertheless, except to one who is a stubborn pessimist, the world seems generally to have improved over the centuries as a place to live in.

Unfortunately, there are some large and powerful groups in the world who disagree violently with this conclusion, or at best preach that people are not reaching their goal of happiness as fast as a beneficent government can give it to them. Whether they be thought of as the forces of evil, jealous, "have nots," misguided reformers, or even saints is relatively unimportant.

What *is* important is the urge among people everywhere to improve the circumstances under which they live. All the peoples of this world want better food, clothing, and shelter; more protection against the hazards of unemployment and old age; proper care should they become sick; security for their families when they die; wider opportunities for education and for growth and development; freedom to do the right things in life; and an improved chance to obtain comfort of both mind and body, and perhaps, happiness.

In those countries that live in liberty these aims and aspirations are highly developed and vocal; the people not only intend to do something about satisfying them, but they have the power to do so.

In our own country we have witnessed a determined effort during the last two decades to realize these aims by political action, that is, to write into law the social reforms which the people as a whole are striving for. The fact that people have turned to politics to satisfy

NOTE: Mr. Babb is President of Lever Brothers and served as Chairman of the Conference on which this book is based.

aspirations which are largely economic in nature shows both that the need is strong and that it has not fully been met by business.

Unfortunately an impression has been built up over the years that many businessmen are selfishly opposed or indifferent to social gains, with the result that the politician has been given a wide-open opportunity to step in as the champion of the people's cause. In this role he has enjoyed the support of many in the fields of education, religion, and social science who recognize the people's wants and who believe any action which aims at satisfying them is good and justifiable.

The businessman, unlike the politician, is naturally cautious about promising more than he can deliver, but he certainly is no opponent of social progress. The whole purpose of business is to satisfy people's wants in the only way they can be satisfied—by more efficient production and distribution.

A few leaders in business have boldly planned their operations with the satisfaction of human aspirations as the major goal. The fact that there have not been enough of them to offset the maneuvers of the politician has not resulted, in my opinion, from any lack of fundamental desire to help people. If this were so, where would all the educational institutions, the hospitals, and the great charity drives have obtained their funds? Rather, I think, it stems from our having too little "know how" about the causes and effects of human motivation.

Over the last half century business has gotten to know the physical sciences, has come to understand their potentials, and has wrought technical improvements far beyond the wildest dreams of our fathers and grandfathers. Perhaps we have all been too busy relishing the fruits of science to spend enough time developing the art of handling people.

There is, I believe, no businessman in this country who will not readily admit that he would rather lose his factories and warehouses and machinery than lose his organization. Yet what proportion of their business hours do businessmen personally spend in the development of people as opposed to the techniques and methods of their jobs? Probably not as much as half of their time.

Why do boards of directors insist on approving capital expenditures for, say, a machine tool costing $10,000 with an expected life of ten years, and at the same time pay little attention to the man who may cost from $100,000 to $1,000,000 over his useful lifetime? Why do we spend our best engineering skills and experience in maintaining, servicing, and oiling a machine in accordance with predetermined standards, and pay so little attention to maintaining, servicing, and oiling the man who runs it?

It seems to me that the main reason is that most of us have not yet understood the economics of happiness. To be sure, we all know that a happy man or woman will do more work and better work than an unhappy person. But, somehow or other, we have difficulty relating that fact to our profits. Rather we tend to think of the things we do to improve the lot of our people as expenses without return. Perhaps because we do, we get less than adequate return from the expenditure. We tend to call such things "fringe benefits," and thereby relegate them to the unimportant.

Too much of our effort in the field of human relations has been expended in a commercial vacuum. If I have any proposition to make, it is that business is a way of life for three out of four people in this country; that people are striving for a good life, liberty, and a chance to attain some degree of happiness in their business association; that if they come reasonably close to reaching their goal, they will be more productive; and if they are more productive, your business and mine will be more profitable.

There are two important corollaries to this proposition. The first is that people who find the satisfactions of life in business will provide poor support to the Communist, or the Socialist, or even the vote-seeking politician who promises a noneconomic route to Utopia. The second is that the advantages of the American way of life will become self-evident to the rest of the peoples of the world who are also seeking a better life, more freedom, and a chance to be a little happier, and we will not have to rely on statistics of bathtub ownership to try to convince them that we have a pretty good thing over here, when what they want is a little more freedom.

Now you will rightly say that happiness in life must be earned;

it cannot be given. This is axiomatic. But let us be realistic, too. The majority of people need leadership. The signposts along the road need to be pretty clear and the obstacles to steady travel toward the destination minimized if the goal is to be reached.

What group is in a better position to take account of the needs and desires of people than the professional managers of business? And who else can make more use of the increased productivity of people?

If anyone is to be responsible for leading the people of this country, and perhaps the world, to greater happiness, and at the same time for making individual businesses more profitable, it should be these professional managers. And if we keep the profit motive uppermost in our minds, where it should be, then what we are describing is how to get people to want to do the things that are important to a healthy business, a sound economy, a free nation, and a better world—because doing those things brings the satisfactions in life which they are seeking.

Now the business of getting people to do things is not a science; it is an art—an art about which we unfortunately know too little. But all the arts are subject to research and analysis, from which certain principles of what is good and what is bad can be developed. The conclusions may not be so exact as those obtainable in mathematics, or chemistry, or physics, but they will be workable concepts.

My company, like many others, has for a number of years sent several men each year to the Advanced Management courses of the Harvard Business School. The major acquisition of the men who complete these courses is a little better understanding of how you get people to do things in business.

This results not from chance or association with men in other businesses but from a very carefully planned and skillfully integrated exposure to the problems of human relations and human motivation, not only in the relatively new course in Administrative Practices but throughout the study of every subject. And this exposure is based on more research and more original thinking on the subject of human motivation in business than has probably ever been attempted by any other institution.

In Part I of this book the Dean of the School and three leaders of business thought will outline some of the problems of "getting things done in business"; and in Part II five panels of Faculty members — 18 in all — will present some of their findings and case material in the same general area. They do not have all the answers on how to make people happy within the framework of the individual company. But they do have some ideas that can be directly and immediately useful to any businessman.

It is to be hoped that as a whole this book will excite the interest of businessmen in the benefits to be gained by doing a better job of getting people to do things; and that as a result each reader individually will devote a little more time and a little more study to the problems of human motivation in his business, with the promise of an economically sound return on the investment.

SELLING IDEAS IN A TROUBLED WORLD

Philip D. Reed

By whatever words one may entitle these observations of mine, the subject seems to boil down to this: How does one get people to do things abroad?

Just as the miracle of mass production is the result of the most intimate study and painstaking selection of every component part, however small, coupled with the integration of many thousands of individual operations into a perfectly timed and synchronized team effort, so any planned effort to influence mass opinion or action must be based on a careful study and a thorough understanding of the individuals who together constitute the mass.

Surely this is an obvious statement and one that we would apply in our own businesses as a matter of course. Product design, advertising, and pricing are based on market surveys, which in the end are analyses of the likes, dislikes, habits, and reactions of a representative group of prospective customers.

So the first and most fundamental guide to fruitful relations with people abroad is: be at great pains to know and understand them. You will perhaps remember one of the hit songs in that delightful musical play, *The King and I,* sung by the English schoolmistress to a group of Siamese children. It is entitled, "Getting to Know You." It makes the point I have in mind and makes it very well.

What is it that motivates people — any and every people?

At the head of the list I would put self-interest. "What's in it for me?" is probably asked more universally and frequently in every language than any other question.

In second place I would put that fine, impulsive human urge to help those who are in trouble. The underdog, the unfairly attacked,

NOTE: Mr. Reed is Chairman of the Board of Directors of the General Electric Company.

the family or region suffering from some catastrophic event beyond its control, all are quick recipients of sympathy and assistance from people everywhere.

And third on my list of human motivations is that old friend of ours, curiosity.

Now, if we are trying to get something done, whether it be selling a mouse trap for profit or creating an organization to build and maintain a peaceful world, we must design our product and present our case in a way to reach and to stir either the self-interest, or the urge to help, or the curiosity, of many people. To put it another way, the product, be it a material object or a great idea, must arouse at least one of those basic impulses.

Assuming, then, that we have successfully selected a product, a project, or an idea, what is the next step in getting people to do things about it? I suggest that it is the selection, orientation, and organization of the team of individuals who will actually present and implement the program. Here again it is easy enough to state the governing rules and principles.

To function effectively, the individuals making up the operating team must understand each other as people and must enjoy mutual respect and confidence. In addition, they must understand precisely what it is that the team is setting out to accomplish, and must believe in the proposed action program for doing the job. This much achieved, there remains to break the project down into clearly defined parts and to assign specific responsibility, authority, and accountability to every member of the team.

No individual task should be too big for a normally competent person to get his arms around. I am convinced that organizations designed for iron men and geniuses are not built for the long pull.

Finally, the team should be headed and led by a person of proven executive ability. I know of no better definition of executive excellence than the one John Hancock of Lehman Brothers gave. He said, "The supreme executive is the man with the greatest ability to influence others to do their best."

So much for fundamentals. My purpose in referring to them was to point out that, whether we are dealing with people at home or abroad, the business of getting them to do things involves the same basic rules and considerations. The additional complications and special problems one finds on the international front are mainly peripheral. It has been my experience, based on rather close association with people from twenty-five countries since World War II, that human beings are very much the same, regardless of color, creed, or nationality.

But what are these differences and special problems? Language, of course, is in most countries a major complication for the average American, including myself. Not to be able to converse in the native tongue of the people one is visiting and working with is to multiply the possibilities of misunderstanding. Differences in customs, conventions, and traditions are also a real but perhaps minor hazard. One must constantly be alert lest offense be given and relations strained quite unintentionally.

Strong nationalistic feelings are, of course, another potential obstacle to international understanding and to acceptance of leadership from another country. Pride, supersensitiveness, and suspicion, fed by a procession of false reports and half-truths about the objectives or conduct of other countries, tend to becloud and chill the atmosphere in which one works.

The very fact of wide physical separation between America and most other countries of the world is a further source of trouble. This would be much less serious if cross-visitation were taking place on a large scale. But it is not. And since there is no substitute for seeing people and places with one's own eyes, we as a nation frequently do not picture things abroad as they really are, nor are we always able to put places and events in proper perspective. The same is equally true, indeed I think more so, of the average foreigner's appraisal of America and Americans. Witness the words of the kindly British parson in a small English village, early in World War II, who said to a friend, "The only Americans I can abide are the ones I have met."

These, then, are some of the additional points that need bearing in mind when one is attempting to make friends and influence people beyond our borders. As I indicated earlier, their importance is real but relative. To deal with them alone would avail us nothing. Our program must be solidly grounded in terms of motivation; and our operating team, be it national or international, must be carefully selected, thoroughly orientated, and soundly organized.

Perhaps I have dealt too much in generalities. Let me try to be a little more specific by saying a few words about two very different kinds of international projects I have been associated with in the past few years.

The first is the Anglo-American Council on Productivity, a body conceived by the late Sir Stafford Cripps, then Chancellor of the Exchequer, and Paul Hoffman, then Administrator of ECA, but organized and operated as a nongovernmental institution. The Council was made up of labor leaders and industrialists from Great Britain and the United States, and its objective was to assist in every possible way to increase the productivity — the output per man-hour — of British industry.

Although Britain has many problems, none is insoluble if she can step up substantially her output per worker-hour. And that it can be done is evidenced by the fact that output per man-hour in the United States is probably two and a half times on the average what it is in Britain.

The story of the work of this Council, which was officially wound up as an international body in London in May 1952, is a long and fascinating one. But I shall limit myself to two brief observations.

First, the goal, the objective of the Council, was so clearly stated and of such vital importance that a very mixed group indeed of British and American labor and industrialist leaders — many of them prima donnas, and some of them probably unable to agree with each other on any other subject — were able in very short order not only to get on a first-name basis with each other but to work harmoniously and effectively during the three and a half years of the Council's existence.

The other point I want to make stems from the fact that, though the importance of the program was well understood at the top, a very significant percentage of British business management and labor leaders did not know, and certainly did not believe, that

American industrial productivity was more than twice that of Great Britain. Furthermore, the resentment in Britain would have been instant and universal had we on the American side undertaken to tell the British what they should do to improve their productivity.

Fortunately, our approach from the beginning was that we did not pretend to know the answers to their problem. We simply invited them to send teams of highly qualified all-British personnel, from as many of their industries as were interested, to visit their counterparts in the United States; to observe our methods, attitudes, and techniques; and to decide for themselves whether any part of what they saw could usefully be adapted to their own industries.

In all, 66 industrial productivity teams, each composing about 15 experts from top management, production, and labor, have since 1948 spent six weeks each, visiting mills and factories. They have issued a series of unanimous all-British reports which — for their penetrating and sometimes brutal self-criticism and for their practical down-to-earth analysis and suggestions for adapting American methods and techniques to their own use — are unique in British industrial history.

The lessons to be drawn from this undertaking are many. It was an encouraging experience for all of us, British and Americans alike, in the field of getting people to do things.

The other international project is very different indeed from the Anglo-American Council. It is an American project currently known as the United States International Information Administration. This organization, as you know, is a part of our Department of State and was authorized by Public Law 402, better known as the Smith-Mundt Act, in 1948. It embraces the use of many media including radio, motion pictures, the press, publications, libraries, and exchange of persons.

As a member of the small Advisory Commission of nongovernmental persons created by the act to confer with the State Department concerning the information program and to report to Congress periodically, I have had a more than ordinary interest in this program and have observed its operation both at headquarters and in the field.

Again, as in the case of the Anglo-American Council on Productivity, I can do no more than touch on two high spots of a great and immensely important undertaking which, I regret to say, is suffering severely from lack of understanding and support on the part both of Congress and of the American people.

First, the information (or propaganda) program got off to a bad start because it did not conform to the basic tests I mentioned at the outset. It offered nothing to the "what's in it for me?" side of the millions of listeners, readers, and viewers abroad; nor did it arouse either the urge to help others or, to any perceptible extent, the curiosity of those it reached.

The reason for this was that, apart from the straight news and entertainment portions of the program, the propaganda was designed to tell the world how fine and generous we Americans are, how much we produce, and how well we live, even those of us in the low-income brackets. The result was that, instead of encouraging foreign audiences to admire, respect, and emulate us, as we had naïvely hoped they would, the stories about automobiles, refrigerators, and washing machines enjoyed by our factory workers either were rejected as blatant falsehoods or so aroused the envy and resentment of those who believed that we found ourselves making more enemies than friends.

I am sure I need not tell you that this phase of the program has been completely recast. If facts about our American way of life are given, they are tailored to the audience and coupled with clear suggestions as to what can be and is being done to adapt these things within the country and for the benefit of the people to whom the program is addressed. In other words, instead of telling people how good we are, we now seek to show them that it is in their own immediate self-interest to turn their backs on Communism and become all-out members of the community of free nations.

The second point that may be worth recording is equally fundamental but, I suspect, less obvious to us Americans than to our friends in foreign lands. We are so thoroughly accustomed to products being unashamedly praised by their makers, so ready to accept the challenge of selling the virtues of our mouse trap as against the product of our competitor, that we sometimes overlook more subtle and frequently more effective techniques.

Take, for example, that great American institution known as the General Electric Company. For some years now we have been widely advertising the statement, "You can put your confidence in General Electric." And we mean every word of it, right down to our toes. But no one can deny that those words, if spoken publicly and repeatedly by a disinterested person or, better still, by a competitor — say, the Westinghouse Company — would carry much more weight, conviction, and punch than when spoken by ourselves. Well, I am bound to confess that the Westinghouse Company has to date shown no strong inclination to shout from the housetops that you can put your confidence in General Electric! Hence, in keeping with the great American traditions of not hiding one's light under a bushel, General Electric itself has been and will continue placing the facts before a friendly and rewarding American public.

Turning back, however, to the foreign front, we have learned by experience that an overpropagandized and therefore cynical people greatly discount any self-serving statement that emanates from government. We have observed, for example, that a pamphlet, strictly objective and truthful in its content, will be far more widely read and willingly believed if attributed to some nongovernmental organization, even though little known, than will an identical pamphlet attributed to the United States Information Service.

Russia has been using this indirect technique with great success for a long while. One may search in vain through tons and tons of Communistic pamphlets, handbills, and publications circulated in Western Europe for one which is attributed to the Russian government or to the Cominform.

Needless to say, the International Information Administration is resorting more and more to the indirect approach, and more and more to the production of its propaganda material in the field rather than here at home.

But these are only the beginnings. Our country is confronted by the realities of an uninvited but imposed leadership of the free world. Many facets of this new role are both unpleasant and unfamiliar to us. We have much to learn. A young man, after graduation, decided to enter the banking business. Within a month or two he was hunting for a new job in an entirely different field, and a friend asked him why he was quitting banking after so short a time. He replied, "I don't like it, and I'm sorry I learned the business."

Things are not quite that simple for us as a nation. Our job of leadership stems from the enormous economic power we possess, and we cannot escape that leadership so long as we retain the power. It behooves us therefore with the greatest seriousness to study and to understand our job. Its complications are almost infinite. It requires action as well as words — action *consistent* with our words. And because our power is grounded on economic strength, the need for a wise and consistent foreign economic policy, including world trade policy, is doubly great. (Yet the fact is that our foreign economic policy has been neither wise nor consistent since we became a creditor nation more than thirty years ago.)

Let me again stress that getting people to do things abroad calls for more than national power or a polished technique. The things we *want* people to do must be sound, consistent, and right things, for them as well as for us.

THE U. S. CORPORATION: A NEW FORM OF GOVERNMENT?

John K. Jessup

We have all been told often enough that American business is under the gun. Here is a contrary message: the gun has been spiked; at any rate one big gun has been spiked for the time being. The gun I speak of is a certain influential portion of public opinion which has been hostile or skeptical toward business management and the free enterprise system for the last twenty years. This gun was forged in the Gilded Age, rifled during several decades of minority discontent, and loaded in the Great Depression, of which it is now a rusting memorial. The crew of this gun was made up of various intellectuals, church groups, professors, and bureaucrats. I need not recall how harassing their fire used to be. It is more instructive to note that it has virtually ceased.

Among these opinion-makers it is no longer taken for granted that the American businessman wields more social power than his economic function or his personal merits entitle him to wield. It is no longer taken for granted that private capitalism is somehow at odds with social justice or with the basic ideals of American democracy. The editors of the *Partisan Review,* who are ex-Marxist but still "avant garde," tell us in a recent issue that American artists and intellectuals, formerly proud of their alienation from our so-called acquisitive society, "have largely come to terms with the realities of the national life." Historians, taking their lead from Allan Nevins, have begun to rehabilitate their old whipping boy, the robber baron, and to ask themselves whether they have not been unjust to American business all along.

For many years the Methodist Church felt that it was part of its Christian duty to tolerate a Federation for Social Action, popularly known as Methodism's "Pink Fringe." This year the Methodist

NOTE: Mr. Jessup is Chief Editorial Writer of *Life*.

General Conference disowned the Federation and also omitted a time-honored slur on the profit motive from the Methodist social creed. With a group as influential and as solidly American as the Methodists, even a slight shift in outlook may have large consequences. Had it not been for the sanction given it by church groups, the Fabian Socialist movement in England might never have got off the ground.

There is a new climate of opinion, as I read it, which is more friendly to our business system and the businessman than it has been in twenty years. I should like first to review the reasons for this new climate, and then to speculate on some of its possible consequences, both for business and for the nation.

The most obvious reasons for the new climate are the long postwar boom and the menace of Soviet Communism. Prosperity and war have always tended to discourage dissident opinion in our society and encourage national unity, whether for good or ill. Another reason is the recent behavior of business leaders, which has been such as to earn public respect. I am not referring to business's increased investment in public relations, nor even necessarily to business's new claims to social responsibility and trusteeship; rather I am thinking of individual businessmen. Business has earned respect partly because it has been infiltrated by men trained to regard it as a profession.

I am also thinking of that remarkable burst of sincere self-appraisal and self-criticism with which even businessmen not so trained began to confront their own future during the late war. An example was the founding of the Committee for Economic Development in 1943, on the then rather daring assumption that the businessman and the academic economist could and should be friends. The CED sessions where this friendship ripened were frequently painful; for, as Paul Hoffman says, there is nothing quite so painful as the sacrifice of a good, healthy prejudice, and at these sessions many prejudices on both sides were cleanly reasoned away. The result is that, by and large, business and economists have a new respect for each other, and this mutual respect has had silent secondary effects in other parts of our university campuses and at the campus periphery, where miscellaneous free-lance intellectuals have felt its force.

Another reason for the spiking of the antibusiness gun is the ruthless way in which recent history has discredited so many naïve "isms" and ideologies. The Soviet spectacle is mainly responsible for this discrediting, being a clear demonstration that a Socialist economy may lead to total political terror. And the English example has added the lesson that even if Socialism does not lead to terror, it certainly does not lead to happiness or wealth. Britain's dependence on aid from capitalist America has undermined the self-confidence of many Socialists both there and here. In a new volume of Fabian essays, Richard Crossman confesses that the Labor Party has exhausted its program and must start rethinking its philosophy.

A few months ago in Cleveland noises could be heard which sounded like the death rattle of the American Socialist Party. This honorable and idealistic little party used to poll nearly a million votes in presidential years, even when its candidate, Norman Thomas, was in jail. This year Norman Thomas did not even attend the convention, having tried to abolish the party two years ago. The New Deal and the Fair Deal have stolen all its issues, and the federal bureaucracy has absorbed most of its personnel.

A two-volume epitaph on *American Socialism* has recently been issued by the Princeton University Press. In it Professor Sidney Hook, himself an intellectual and something of a Socialist, asks why Socialism never got very far in the United States. Here is part of his answer:

> Socialism made little headway because the philosophy of Americanism itself was a kind of . . . "surrogate" socialism. Socialism promised a classless society in the future. Americanism taught that the citizens of the United States already enjoyed it in the present. Socialism celebrated it not only as part of "the American Dream" but boasted that its evidences were everywhere at hand. Socialism promised a release of productive forces. Americanism pointed to the country's rising standard of living: there were no limitations upon economic productivity, except temporary ones. Socialism preached the gospel of freedom and equality. These were the familiar shibboleths of the mythology of Americanism, reinforced by legend, history, and actual fact. At every point Socialism encountered

the obstacle of a prior faith which was so much like it in aspiration, promise, even in phrasing, that to substitute the first for the second seemed to be pointless.

In other words, America's actual economic and social performance has outraced the imagination of its Utopian critics. Our business civilization has not only contradicted their prophecies but exhausted their dreams.

This of course does not mean that American business is beyond criticism, or that it is without domestic enemies. The Fair Deal, of course, warmed up the old antibusiness slogans again, though they did not prove to be as effective politics in 1952 as they were in 1948. But the point is that a former enemy of business, what we might term the intellectually respectable branch of the political left, no longer takes these slogans seriously. It is not only newly tolerant of our business system but somewhat in awe of it.

In awe, yes, and also mystified. Here is an economy, still predominantly capitalist, that has gone through a metamorphosis, or perhaps a revolution, for which none of the familiar tools of ideological analysis afford an adequate explanation. Not only the Marxian but even the ethical tools turn in the honest critic's hand. If ours can still be called an acquisitive society, it is so in a different sense from what R. H. Tawney meant when he invented the phrase. Still more puzzling is the question of "the bosses." Who really disposes of final economic power? Two key examples will show why the intellectual is puzzled, as anyone must be who aspires to schematic thinking about the American political economy today.

First, consider the modern corporation. Who really runs it, and in whose behalf? Certainly its owners do not run it, nor is it run primarily *for* the stockholders. Is it run, then, by and for the new managerial class? Or is that class merely the servant of those many rival claimants — stockholders, customers, employees, competitors, suppliers — whose conflicting interests management must consult and compose?

Scarcely less puzzling is the economy as a whole. The ownership of the means of production, which Marx thought all-important, is clearly less important than other incentives to production in determining our level of prosperity The federal budget is now the most important single factor in the economy; and when it comes to redistributing income, neither labor unions nor the farm bloc, nor any other lobby, is half so potent as the progressive income tax.

These are measurable facts But what is not measurable is the source of control over these big facts. Who really determines the level of our budget and the incidence of our taxes? Is it Stalin, or Truman, or Lovett, or Muley Doughton, or Senator George, or the press, or the lobbies, or the folks back home? No analyst of power feels too sure. One sociologist David Riesman, complains that the present power pattern of United States society has become utterly amorphous and mercurial; power resists attempts to locate it or measure it just as an atom, by Heinenberg's principle of uncertainty, defies simultaneous efforts to ascertain its position and velocity.

No wonder so many intellectuals have deserted political and economic theory for the hazy new categories of sociology. Their plight recalls the story of the girl who visited a psychiatrist to tell him about her brother, who was about to become his patient. The girl wanted to give the psychiatrist a little background on what she felt was an unusual case.

"My brother is under the illusion that he is a hen," she said. "He goes around clucking; he picks up sand and stuff with his teeth."

"How long has he had this illusion?" asked the psychiatrist.

"About twelve years," she replied.

"Twelve years!" he exclaimed, "and you haven't consulted a doctor before now?"

"Well, up till now," said the girl, "we've always been able to use the eggs."

I maintain, however, that there is no need to consult a psychiatrist or even a sociologist. What we have here is a real hen and a problem in political economy. The age-old truths and insights of that traditional science are still our best approach to understanding this new American revolution and guessing where it will take us next.

A generation ago the late Charles Beard pointed out that the

American Constitution, like other sensible political documents, was firmly based in private economic interests. For this he was roundly denounced as a Marxist, although his actual sources were Aristotle, John Locke, *The Federalist* papers, and Daniel Webster. Without a firm economic base, said Beard, "political science cannot rise much above the level of astrology"; for unless and until the Army takes over, economic forces are a pretty safe guide to politics, though of course not the only one.

This was crystal clear to the framers of our Constitution. Since they saw the American task as the preservation of liberty, they were concerned with protecting the right to property as basic to liberty, and they saw that their best chance lay in the widespread ownership of land which gave voters an economic stake in their own freedom. It was the colonists' self-owned and self-worked land, as Webster said later, that "fixed the future frame and form of their government." Madison in addition, in *The Federalist* papers, argued that the diffusion of political power among a "multiplicity of factions," or conflicting interest groups, was the best guarantee that no easy majority of the underprivileged would ever combine to use the Federal Government for purpose of pillage.

This theory of balanced and diffused economic power is deeply embedded in American political theory and history, much more deeply than, for example, the merely legal concept of states' rights. As Beard put it, the "founding fathers" were concerned with property rights as well as abstract rights, because they wanted to protect "the real rights of real people."

When Beard in 1945 tried to update his *Economic Basis of Politics,* he cautiously predicted that "if history is any guide, drastic changes in the economy will find expression in politics," and vice versa. But he was unable to analyze the exact nature of the drastic economic changes which have in fact occurred.

For purpose of argument, let us think of these changes in terms of what has been called the "organizational revolution."

Most American citizens now work not on farms but in industrial groups, of which the archetype is the modern corporation. Most of us are employees; as individuals we may own a lot of property, but usually not the property that gives us our livelihood. Nor is the corporation's ownership of physical property—plant and machinery—the only reason we work for it. We work for it because the organization itself, not what it owns, has become the real unit of production. That, it seems to me, is the genuine novelty in our revolution. For economic purposes the organization is more important than what it owns or who works for it. It has a life of its own. What began as a mere legal person has acquired a social personality.

Now let us ask what is the chief political problem before Americans today? It may well be a moral and spiritual problem, transcending economic solutions. It is certainly part of a world problem, the struggle with Communism. But that struggle creates a subsidiary problem for Americans which is purely domestic and morally neutral: how to survive and win this struggle as a garrison state without putting our essential liberties in the hands of our government.

Thus stated, the problem is exactly what it was in 1787: how to protect the liberties of American citizens against the tendency of government to grow too strong, to become a leviathan instead of a limited state, to substitute what some think is good government for what all know is self-government—a tendency that is true of all governments including our own.

Governor Adlai Stevenson of Illinois, whose own party has been sailing on "the great tidal drift toward monistic and mammoth government," urges us all to "paddle vigorously against the stream" and to erect "dikes against the flood waters sweeping toward the District of Columbia." The dikes he has in mind are stronger and better state and local governments—a proposition with which few will quarrel. The more power the states can keep, the better.

But even in 1787 Hamilton called the states a mere "administrative convenience," and today they are not so much a sanctuary of sovereignty as a source of senators. The economic base of their power ebbs and flows, but not even Texas is truly sovereign in an economic sense. Even in so simple a case as the tidal oil lands, where both Congress and the oil are on their side, the states have the greatest difficulty maintaining their rights against the Federal Government; and, instead of a great Constitutional issue, this one became a tangle of lobbyists and lawyers.

Now look at another case which did become a great Constitutional issue. It arose when the President — in the name of the world crisis — seized the steel industry. This electrified the country and even aroused the Supreme Court. Due process, Fifth Amendment, emergency powers, these were all in the briefs; if he can seize your steel mill without statutory authority, what is to prevent him from seizing my home?

Yet I doubt very much whether most people felt that private property was the electrifying element in this crisis. Industrial property is not private in John Locke's sense of an extension of the person. No, what disturbed people about the steel case was not the invasion of property but the invasion of what was, and what should be, an area of industrial self-government. They were shocked at the hint that our great organizational revolution might have rendered steel permanently incapable of self-government, that the White House might have to make the major steel decisions forever.

In short, the basic right now called in question by the world crisis is the right of self-government. Within the United States, that right needs a newly defined economic base. I suggest that many of the present vague fears and psychic uncertainties of the American people would vanish if they had a good economic reason to believe that theirs is still a limited state, a federal republic. People differ greatly as to when and whether their rights have been transgressed. But these differences are minor compared with the question of whether they have, as a people, some assurance that the Federal Government will not itself be the final arbiter of those rights. Neither states' rights nor the laws of property can adequately supply this assurance any longer.

To give this assurance, to fill this economic vacuum in our federal republic, I nominate the modern corporation. To make the case fully, and with all the necessary hedging, would require a very long nominating speech indeed. I will confine myself to three salient characteristics of the corporation which seem to qualify it for this important political office.

In the first place, the corporation is today our chief source of national wealth. It is our most characteristic way of mobilizing men and resources and organizing work. In this respect its "inherent" powers are less disputable than those of the Presidency. Any President who wants to run a prosperous country depends on the corporation at least as much as, and probably more than, the corporation depends on him. His dependence is not unlike that of King John on the landed Barons of Runnymede where Magna Charta was born. The corporation is a focus of real economic power. It should therefore be capable of limiting and offsetting what has been called the Federal Government's increasing "efficiency of coercion." This is one political asset of the corporation.

In the second place, the corporation and the business system in which it lives are friendly to certain homely virtues which are not only good in themselves but are thought good by most Americans. Kenneth Boulding's article in the April–May 1952 *Harvard Business Review* describes the "ethic of capitalism." Among its more obvious virtues are efficiency, thrift, and honesty — virtues which the voters do not always find in their government but which the business world harbors and perpetuates because they are the laws of its being. Among our institutions which a strong government is most inclined to tamper with and to politicize are the value of the dollar and the predictability of the law. Business has a strong interest in both a predictable dollar and predictable laws. So have the people in the long run. The fact that business stands for these social virtues and valued institutions may on some near occasion make business their political champion, which could be a popular cause.

In the third place, without any sacrifice of its strong economic base, the corporation is fast taking on many new social responsibilities. The practicing businessman knows what these new responsibilities are and how far they may be expected to go. The fact that the corporation promises to become a sort of welfare community is the best guarantee that we need not have a national welfare state.

The intellectuals used to make one very serious charge against private capitalism — namely, that it makes for an atomized society, replacing genuine communities with a mere "cash nexus." The corporation, as Peter Drucker has pointed out, is repairing this damage and making the charge obsolete. Corporation members are not economic atoms; they are part at least of a very large molecule.

The internal life of the corporation is a new frontier, and like the old physical frontier, it can be a fresh fountain of democracy. The chief social tensions of our industrial age, including even the fear of unemployment, are those which arise from the new relation of man to his work. The corporation therefore harbors and confronts practically all these tensions; and the more it resolves them for the sake of its own survival, the more it will have resolved them for society as well.

Thus the corporation has a major and growing role in the political economy of a free nation. It is not an exclusive role. There are many other results of the "organizational revolution," from labor unions to the WCTU, and many of these, like the states and cities, are vital organs of American self-government. Moreover, our politics are ultimately ruled not by economic but by ethical considerations, and these will limit, although they need not disparage, the corporation's role in our civilization. But its chief business after all is business. So long as it succeeds at that, it will fill the American need for a focus of self-government with an economic base.

In its early days the corporation needed no extra social sanction for the permission to exist which the law gave it. It was adequately sanctioned, and so were its profits, by being subject to a competitive market.

More recently the labor movement has placed an additional check on corporate management's freedom of maneuver. Both these checks will continue. In taking on new responsibilities, management should not expect to win any new managerial freedoms. The more responsibility it undertakes, the more society will ask of it. In short, the more nearly impossible will the corporate manager's job become.

But one annoyance, at least, he can count on leaving behind. This is the harassing criticism of those who have hitherto doubted management's very title to manage. This title may still be legally clouded, but the political cloud on it is lifting.

For evidence of this, consider some basic opinions which most American business managers have long held in common. One is that rising productivity is the key to prosperity. This is now a commonplace of general opinion as well. Another is that labor and capital, consumers and vendors, big business and small, all share an interest in rising productivity, and that our industrial society is therefore founded on a harmony of classes, not a conflict. This view too commands general assent.

The public is also aware that the torch for these hopeful truths has been carried in recent years not by labor, and not by government, and not by intellectuals, but by American business management. The public opinion I speak of is, therefore, just about ready to admit an additional proposition: namely, that of all the interest groups that influence business decisions, management on its recent record has the best claim to disinterestedness and intelligence and hence the best claim to the last word in those decisions. Management is earning the title Colby Chester gives it: "the court of fair rewards."

Public opinion is fickle. The right to manage is not only a severely limited right, but one that must be earned afresh with every political generation. Moreover, if my thesis is correct, this right to manage may begin to carry an extra political charge, as people come to acknowledge the corporation's political role.

Just what does all this imply for business managers? Their role does sound portentous. In addition to all they do now, must they become professional politicians as well? No, not in any unpleasant sense of the word. The manager's political function, as I see it, is simply to keep proving in the future what he has already begun to prove; namely, that the corporation is a new, vital kind of commonwealth within which individual citizens can work to produce wealth in harmony and to share it in a spirit of practical justice. As chief of this little commonwealth, the manager has the political job of keeping all his constituents reasonably happy in that part of their lives which relates to their work. Success in that objective makes the corporation successful.

To "get people to do what you want them to do" — at least in a free country — you must of course want them to do what is in their own real interest. Modern management has shown that it understands this. It knows how to find a genuine identity between the interest of the corporation as a whole and the interests of its members as individuals. That is quite an achievement. And all I am saying is that this achievement may be even more important than you think. For there is a further identity of interest between a well-run corporation and a well-organized nation.

Let me summarize as follows. In doing its economic job so well, American business has shown how certain economic conflicts, which were getting dangerously and unnecessarily involved in national politics, can be solved by the older methods of private self-government, and can therefore be legitimately kept out of the federal orbit. In doing this job, business is erecting a new basis of economic power which is beyond the reach of government, thus helping to preserve freedom.

A nation whose structure includes a multiplicity of healthy self-governing economic units will still have plenty of big national political worries. But they will be more consistent with freedom and more manageable by democratic means.

LIBERTY AND THE PURSUIT OF HAPPINESS IN BUSINESS

Franklin J. Lunding

"How to get people to do things" is perhaps the most important question facing business management today. It is a problem for which there is no set of easy answers.

Without doubt, people are inspired to do things more by spiritual than by material considerations. There is virtually no limit to their ability to accomplish outstanding results when they work together under the inspiration of something in which they all believe. Let their country's safety be threatened, let their community interests be in jeopardy, let their team be in danger of losing, and they rise to the occasion, often at the cost of considerable personal effort and with little hope of gain. They can manage, after a day's work, to put more energy, spirit, and enthusiasm into a session of bowling or softball than they put into their jobs. They run themselves ragged in pursuit of a sport or a hobby. These after-hours activities seldom yield anything of a tangible nature, and yet people give to such activities "all they have got." Obviously, it takes something more than the lure of money to inspire people to do their best and give their all.

Our problem is to identify and harness this psychological stimulus in order to induce people to display the same interest and energy in their daily work.

It comes down, I think, to a question of fundamentals in human nature. People go "all out" for those things they enjoy and in which they believe. It is necessary for business management to win for the company some degree of that belief, loyalty, and devotion which people give to their team, their community, or their country.

This all leads up to my main theme. There is a lesson to be drawn from the basic principles of human relations embodied in the

NOTE: Mr. Lunding is Chief Executive Officer of the Jewel Tea Company.

Declaration of Independence and the Constitution. These principles, and the rights assured by these documents, are responsible on the national scale for the greatest release of human ingenuity and energy in the world's history. Every immigrant to our shores comes here in search of these rights and with the knowledge that in this land his rights are guaranteed by law and respected by all the people. Because Americans have felt secure in these rights and agree generally on what they are, they work together to uphold them. They accept the proposition that vying for individual advantage must not transgress the rights of others.

Their loyalty and devotion to their country spring from a common devotion to these principles; and, when the nation's interests are at stake, they put aside antagonisms and work together for a common purpose.

This truth suggests that in "getting people to do things" a primary task of business management is to apply this same proven concept to economic activity. It should be possible to provide in the business organization the equivalent of what the Constitution and the Bill of Rights provide politically so that people will be more united in furthering a proposition in which they all have a stake.

Such a goal, in my opinion, may best be achieved by introducing much more American democracy into industry in a way which recognizes that the real masters are the consumers and that both the employers and the employed are servants of the community and, therefore, in the same boat.

This brings us to the question: What is democracy as we know it in America — as we have seen it practiced from our humble beginnings? The most important lessons we have been taught seem to me to be about as follows:

1. People in the U. S. A. make their own laws through their elected representatives.
2. People in the U. S. A. have a say in the administration of these laws.
3. People in the U. S. A. are protected by impartial courts of justice.
4. People in the U. S. A. are at liberty to criticize the government either by word of mouth or in writing.
5. People in the U. S. A. are further protected by the Bill of Rights against arbitrary action by any branch of government or any person.

These principles of our democratic republic can be introduced into business to raise standards of performance in the public interest. Democratic principles can form the basis for a philosophy which will be understood and supported by every member of a business organization and which will help convince him that he, too, is an important part of his company and that his welfare and security will advance if the business operates more efficiently.

The internal laws in a business organization are the working and policy rules. Before unions reached positions of power, these normally were developed exclusively by management and posted on the bulletin boards. All were expected to live up to them without question. There was little opportunity to help make them more effective or to protest against unfairness. Written or spoken criticism often was resented by management and sometimes resulted in loss of livelihood for those who expressed themselves too openly. For all practical purposes the lives and well-being of many persons were in the hands of the rulers of business empires.

Obviously, this state of affairs could not be borne forever by a people becoming more and more versed in the ways and rights of a democracy. The pendulum swung the other way as the people made their will felt through the channels of their political power. In the past twenty years, with government encouragement, the dictatorial powers held at one time by the business managers have been transferred in large measure to the labor leaders.

This situation has brought strife and bitterness in broad areas of our economic life, due, I think, to the obvious fact that the claims of employees often are pressed vigorously in violation of the rights of others who play essential parts in the economic activities of a free society.

Shareowners have rights, too, which must be respected if the business is to prosper; they are entitled to a reasonable return on their investment if the enterprise is successful. So do customers have rights; they are entitled to share in the fruits of improved technology through lower prices for better products. Finally, management itself has rights which are no less important; it is entitled to manage without undue interference or harassment and should have the trust and confidence of shareowners, employees, and customers.

Such trust and confidence, of course, must be earned by management through its attitude and performance. It must manage well and at the same time master the art of balancing the rights and interests of customers, employees, and shareowners so that there is no unfair encroachment by one upon the other.

This latter responsibility is perhaps the most important one which present-day management carries. It is impossible to get people to do things unless they feel they are being treated fairly. It is impossible to develop an enthusiastic, smooth-running organization which operates to maximum effectiveness when vital elements are disgruntled or nurse a feeling of injustice.

Perhaps it is well to pause at this point to bring up to date our picture of management.

Under our present system business managers are being chosen by a process of natural selection. More and more, the ownership of our larger companies is becoming fragmented among the general public. Under such conditions the shareholders and employees alike — and in many instances employees are shareholders, too — are interested in getting the best and most efficient management. In most circumstances inherited ownership, even when it represents a sizable portion of the total, is no longer able to take command of a company's destiny unless it first proves its superior ability to do so.

Thus, there has arisen in this country a profession of business management, to which schools of business contribute immeasurably. What sort of men are these managers? What motivates them? What are their goals?

In most cases they are men who have come up through business; who have learned as they went along and who, by successfully discharging lesser responsibilities, have progressed on to major ones. Not even graduates of schools of business administration start in at the top. They may never get there, either, unless with their training they bring intelligence, judgment, courage, determination, and a liking for hard work.

It can be said without qualification that the typical business manager of America today is not working primarily to get rich. In the first place, that is virtually impossible, at least in the formerly accepted sense of the word, and the business manager knows it. No matter how high his salary rises, he is not going to become an immensely wealthy man under present tax laws. Furthermore, he would be likely to find great wealth embarrassing, even if he could acquire it. The opulence which characterized the great business leaders of bygone years is out of place today.

The chief motivation of today's business manager is a desire to build a sound, healthy organism, financially strong, competitively alert, able to progress steadily and to weather whatever storms might lie ahead. His objective is a smooth-running, tight-knit, coöperative organization to which everyone from the president to the floor sweeper contributes his enthusiastic best and from which each draws his due share of material reward and spiritual satisfaction.

Such an organization, the manager is convinced, operates more profitably and offers the best prospects for steady jobs at good pay, for the growth and development of the business and of each individual in it, and for the pursuit of happiness and life's satisfactions for all concerned. The business manager wants all these things for the people who work in the business as much as they want them for themselves. His primary job is to get people to do things coöperatively so that those goals may be achieved.

When the basic rights enjoyed by Americans, as offered in the check list I mentioned previously, are applied in business, management is well on the way to attaining the objectives sought. To illustrate how this may be done, I should like now to cite a "case history" from my own experience, if only because businessmen are always more interested in specifics than in generalities.

On March 12, 1932, slightly over twenty years ago, the Jewel Tea Company purchased 81 retail outlets all located in the Chicago market and overnight became an operator of chain grocery stores. This was a brand-new venture, entirely different from the company's previous business. To operate these stores we employed outside management, experienced in the retail grocery business but, unfortunately, with little understanding of human relations and no feeling for basic American rights. There was no wholehearted participation by employees and no possible reason for interest on their part other than the need to get a few dollars at the end of the week for their modest living. The fear of losing their jobs was the only incentive they had. As a consequence, for reasons beyond the hard, economic limitations of the depression, this venture was anything but successful.

The brutal results appeared in red ink at the bottom of the profit and loss statement. We had to do something about this new business of ours, or else liquidate it. This forced the regular Jewel management to step in and take an active part in the effort to save a sinking ship.

One of the first important actions was the establishment of joint consultation between management and the rank and file of the employees through an employee representation plan. The make-up of this group gave employee representatives a numerical advantage of about five-to-one over management representatives. Any question, substantial or trivial, was eligible for the agenda.

The early meetings were long and took infinite patience, but we soon were able to chart the vast areas of employee dissatisfaction. Confidence grew fast when it was demonstrated that management intended to give the employees the facts about the business and to call on them for help in making it a success. Full minutes of all meetings were kept and distributed to all employees. Everyone in the business knew what was going on in these meetings, what decisions were reached, and the reasons for reaching them. Never once did we find it impossible to arrive promptly at a decision without a dissenting vote. Never once did anyone show even a disposition to be unfair.

Then came the Wagner Act. It declared employee representation plans to be employer-dominated and therefore illegal.

Next came a surprise. Our employee representatives retained an outside attorney and formed their own independent union. This union is still very much active, having won an election for certification conducted by the Labor Board. Its membership under its charter is restricted to those employed in our stores in all departments except meats; meat department employees are represented by the AFL. There has never been any friction between these two unions, and their members have worked in our stores side by side in harmony for years.

I do not wish to create the illusion that the officers of this independent union are, or ever have been, easy negotiators. They know the business, and they have their ideas as to what it can pay. They know what it takes to please customers, who have the free choice of going elsewhere for their food purchases. They also know what competition can do to our stores if we get out of line in our prices or policies. They retain experienced legal talent to advise them of their rights.

Out of all this has grown a further joint effort. Each year, following the completion of negotiations, the independent union and the company prepare, print, and distribute a booklet entitled, "One-Third of Your Life." The title reflects the time we spend on our jobs. The booklet describes company objectives, employee benefits, contract terms both as to hours and as to pay, and how and where to register grievances and secure prompt settlement. This booklet is given to all grocery employees including the new members of our organization. In addition, copies of the union contract itself are available in each store.

I am especially proud of this particular joint effort. It proves that people in our business help make their own laws and that they have a say in the administration of these laws. They can complain and get justice if their dissatisfaction has merit. They are not denied participation in the affairs of their company.

Some may think that this is all fine and that such a joint effort is possible with an independent union representing only the employees of a single company, but how is joint consultation possible with employees who are members of a strong, outside, industry-wide union? I should like to take a few moments to describe recent relationships with our truck drivers.

Until October 1, 1951, all deliveries of merchandise from our warehouses to stores were handled by a contract carrier. As of that date we leased his trucks, and his union employees went on our payroll. Early in February, some five months after this changeover, we started weekly clinics with our drivers. These are conducted informally and give us the opportunity to explain our ideas for improving each operation. The drivers, in turn, tell us whether they think our ideas will work. If in their opinion our proposals seem impractical, we solicit their suggestions for improvement. We are willing to try any reasonable suggestion they may make. As a result, we are constantly trying something different to bring about better service, better working conditions, and lower costs. Obviously, we want a full eight hours' work, five days each week, for every man and all equipment; but we do not want to take advantage of the men.

What has happened since these clinics were started? Our grocery managers tell us our drivers are coöperative and interested. The drivers tell us the people in the stores are helping them do a better job, and they indicate in many ways that they are more satisfied with their jobs. The officers of the truck drivers' union (it is affiliated with the AFL) know of these clinics and their purpose. They are held with the union's consent.

Such "what do you think?" clinics are used constantly all through the company. Managers, cashiers, clerks—all have a chance to comment on operations and offer ideas for improvement.

In dealing with people, both organized and unorganized, we find we can get democracy in business through joint consultation with employees except in those instances where employees are members of unions which insist on industry-wide contract negotiations. Under such circumstances, it is difficult to achieve coöperation that is pointed completely toward improvements in our effort to serve the public and to make our company a better place in which to work. Short-term, selfish interest gets far more attention than long-term, public interest. Unfortunately, an alert, progressive, democratic business and its employees are limited in what they can do by resistance to change which comes from outside the company.

Where there are no monopolies, the desire to serve customers better through improved methods and to get ahead of competition provides the fuel that lets the engine respond when you step on the accelerator. Unless incentive is stifled by monopoly or otherwise, most of us have hidden within us the desire to participate as full-fledged, well-paid members of a winning team.

The job of getting people to do things is never ending and has many facets. For example, we are often inclined to resist doing things for people which, it might be argued, they should do for themselves. On the other hand, as professional managers, we must realize that people cannot give proper attention to jobs if their minds are full of worries. Thus it is wise to try to isolate the big worries of the head of a family and to see if they can be eliminated through joint consultation and coöperative action. Typical among such worries are the following:

How will I support my family if I get sick or suffer a disabling accident?

How can I pay the doctor and hospital bills if misfortune strikes me or my family?

What happens to my family if I die?

What will happen to me when I have to retire?

In our company we have tried to answer these uncertainties or worries by a package plan that was initially started in 1938 and has been constantly improved since. This package plan provides sick compensation for six months; hospital, surgical, and medical benefits; group life insurance; and a retirement estate built jointly by employee savings and participation in the company's profits. These protections, plus unemployment benefits, social security, and workmen's compensation, help overcome most of the worries which detract from efficiency on the job.

Our plans are contributory. The great lesson we have learned out of our experience with contributory plans is that people not only are willing to help provide for themselves but seem to feel better if they do. We have also found that people want to save in a regular way under a program which makes it difficult for them to dissipate the security "nest egg" their savings have built.

In Jewel we are learning to use a technique which we call "sharing the business" to solve all sorts of problems in all departments.

Instead of *telling* our people what to do to solve their problems, we are placing ourselves at their disposal to lend what assistance we can to help them find their own solutions, and we are *asking* them to give us the benefit of their thinking and help us solve our problems.

In other words, we are eliminating the concept of management by edict or handing down orders from an "ivory tower." We have developed what we call the "first assistant" philosophy. Each one of our executives is asked to consider that he works as the first assistant to the next person in line *below* him. He begins by developing an understanding with himself that he does not run the business but assists those who do. He tries to forget that he is boss and to remember that any prestige that he might have comes from what he can accomplish for others rather than from the symbols of his office.

Each executive is charged not so much with the directing and supervising of people as with offering and giving assistance to those who look to him for leadership. Each is asked to think of himself not as a boss but as first assistant to those who report to him. The practical effect of this "first assistant" philosophy is to turn the organization chart upside down with each executive feeling that his job is to help the next man up the line on the upside-down chart.

In our company, responsibility has been delegated to the department heads assigned to the various functions and activities of the business. Each then spends his time helping subordinates with their decisions, advancing suggestions, keeping them informed of what is going on in other departments, studying underlying trends, and in general applying himself to improving the climate in which the entire organization lives and works. This is true from the chief executive officer on down; the same approach is applied throughout the various executive and supervisory levels of the company.

This type of approach recognizes the fact that there is a phantom ballot going on all the time among the people in any business. They vote constantly in their minds for or against their supervisors. Favorable votes show up in coöperation, teamwork, understanding, and production. To keep winning this phantom ballot, each supervisor must share each group's problems with its members and work tirelessly for them instead of trying to make them work for him.

In the final analysis, I think, every organization takes its cue from the character and personality of the man or men at the top. The quality of leadership is the greatest factor influencing the organization's performance. Before we can achieve outstanding success in getting people to do things, we must formulate a personal code of leadership and subscribe to it in our hearts and minds as well as in our official pronouncements.

Such a code might contain the following elements:

1. A realization that the foundation of business success is the confidence which springs from integrity, fair dealing, and mutual benefit for all who participate in business.

2. A belief that business exists to create goods and provide services beneficial to the community and that it should pursue no policies detrimental to the general welfare.

3. A belief that employees are entitled to as good pay for their services as the business can afford and all possible opportunities for advancement, security, and fruitful, satisfying lives.

4. A belief that the customers of a business are entitled to depend on it to keep its promises, to rely on the specified quality of its product, and to share fairly in the fruits of progress through better products at lower prices.

5. A belief that the owners are entitled to a fair return on their investment if the enterprise is successful, plus an increase in the value of their equity if the company grows and prospers; that their property right in the business is a human right no less than any other human right.

6. A realization that the well-being of a large number of people is wrapped up in the business and that management's decisions must always be taken with their welfare in mind.

7. An awareness that an inescapable responsibility of a business organization is to become and remain a source of economic strength to the community and the nation, and not a source of weakness and instability.

8. A belief that no man should be content to seek financial success for itself, but that the moral values of life should dominate his thinking and his actions; that the Golden Rule is still the best and soundest business principle.

Business managers always must be aware, I think, that they are dealing with human beings and that human beings enthusiastically follow leadership which they respect and admire. They must realize also that there is no such thing as an average person and that every individual is different from every other. It is those leaders with the wisest heads and the biggest hearts who will be most successful in getting people to do things.

This does not mean that in handling their affairs business managers should be softhearted or "do gooders," but rather that in dealing with people they be guided by the following advice from Tolstoy:

> It all lies in the fact that men think there are circumstances when one may deal with human beings without love; and there are no such circumstances. One may deal with things without love; one may cut down trees, make bricks, hammer iron, without love; but you cannot deal with men without it, just as one cannot deal with bees without being careful. If you deal carelessly with bees, you will injure them, and will yourself be injured. And so with men.

DEVELOPING ADMINISTRATIVE CONCEPTS IN BUSINESS

Donald K. David

The accomplishment of the world's work is the essence of the administrative process. The Harvard Business School is a school of administration, fortunate in its title and in the vision which foresaw the direction of its development. Our traditional concentration on administration has led us to explore many of the questions which underlie today's concern with the role of people in the administrative process. So perhaps it will be appropriate to review some of the past work of the School and to predict where we may well go in the years ahead.

As I think about what has been going on here, I am impressed by one occurrence in particular. To our oldest and still essential objective — the training of students for *competent performance in business* — we have added the study of the *responsibilities of management.* The sense of obligation we hope to kindle in the men who study business in one of the schools of a great university is twofold:

1. On the one hand, it extends to the people who make up our thousands upon thousands of companies. It means providing for them not only the conditions essential to the effective performance of work but to the realizing of their potentialities as persons. In this connection, the relationship between the satisfactions a person derives from his work and the spontaneous productiveness which such satisfactions necessarily involve means that today's theme might better have been phrased "*allowing* people to do things" rather than "*getting* people to do things." Providing the conditions within which people will themselves decide to accomplish as much as they can is more fruitful than trying to "get" people to work despite unremoved obstacles.

2. But another responsibility we have tried to learn about has extended beyond the achievement of coöperation *within* a company. We have come to see that a businessman has obligations outside his company — obligations to his community, to the country comprised of all such communities,

NOTE: Mr. David is Dean of the Harvard Graduate School of Business Administration.

and to a world of interdependent free men. Our ideas about administration have thus expanded to add to business ability a sense of responsibility to individual and social progress. Before exploring the direction of our future development, I should like to look with you very briefly first at our work in Human Relations and then at our attempt to define social responsibility.

Shortly after I came to the School in 1942, it became a military academy, training mostly servicemen. The Advanced Management Program was foreshadowed in the retraining of businessmen for the rigors of war production.

Beginning years before, Dean Wallace B. Donham, Elton Mayo, and L. J. Henderson had formulated out of early physiological and psychological experiments in the Fatigue Laboratory and the classic Western Electric experiments a new discipline now called Human Relations. The war, rather than stopping this work, gave it new impetus; for emergency emphasized the human problems in industry and made them obviously urgent. Younger colleagues of the three great men I mentioned — Fritz Roethlisberger, George Lombard, and John Fox — studied such questions as absenteeism and turnover in the aircraft industry, and Mayo himself became very much involved in homefront wartime problems. Meanwhile, under the inspirational leadership of Dean Donham, Drs. Arlie Bock, David Dill, John Talbot, William Forbes, and others in the Fatigue Laboratory continued their studies of the effects of cold, heat, altitude, and fatigue which were of immediate and urgent interest to the armed services.

While experimentation and study were carried on in defense factories and in the laboratory, many members of the Faculty helped bring these findings into the classroom. Early courses in Human Relations culminated after the war, under the leadership of a group of men headed by Professor Learned, in a first-year course called Administrative Practices. This course asks students in the Master of Business Administration and the Advanced Management programs to consider the implications of getting things done not in a vacuum but in organizations of real people. Professors Roethlisberger and Lombard with their colleagues developed other courses for our second-year program, for Radcliffe's Management Training Program, and, together with Dean Donham, for the General Education program in Harvard College.

With the development of the new postwar curriculum, Mayo's pioneering work has therefore been blended with the School's long-time practice of concrete consideration of problem after problem in the interest of getting things done in business organizations. The course in Administrative Practices is now an important part of the School's curriculum and research program.

Out of these developments has come a permanently enlarged concept of administration. So long as business decisions are formulated and carried out in groups of people, then the contribution of people to business is a vital concern of the administrator. Attitudes appropriate to effective administration now include a willingness to consider and provide for the demands of individuals upon their organizations, to provide not only a livelihood but a satisfactory way of life, to furnish the opportunity for individual growth and dignity, and to make available at work some of the same satisfactions available to a free citizen elsewhere in his life.

Responsibility toward people in an organization is not designed just to get work from them. Rather it is clear that management cannot preside over a "society" without acknowledging obligations to (as well as contributions from) its members. The School discovered for itself, then, that to train men in business includes training men in the attitudes, abilities, and knowledge which enable them to work with other people. Certainly the School has found a growing recognition of "administration by consent."

Now the discovery that an executive works with a community even within his own company has led us naturally enough into the broader area of relationships between business and other segments of society. A second outgrowth of the new postwar curriculum — in addition to Administrative Practices — has been a required first-year course called Business Responsibilities and the American Society. As the world rolled on, it became inevitable that no one could study business without studying the relationship of business to government, of individual businesses to their community, of businesses (in a competitive system) to each other.

As we attempt to clarify what we mean by social responsibility, we try to make our students aware of the legal, economic, and political environment within which business decisions are made. We hope they will learn *how* (not necessarily *what*) to think about the impact of their behavior as individual businessmen and as members of the business world upon their community. We hope they will begin to formulate their own ideas of competition and will begin to consider what businessmen as distinguished from government administrators can do to contribute to the stability of our economy. We would like them to be able to discriminate between practices which are in the public interest and those which are not. The cases discussed and debated in class are designed to call into the spotlight the scope of the public responsibilities which businessmen must fulfill as the corollary to the freedoms in making business decisions which our economic system affords.

So administration includes not only the relationships among people in a given company but the relationships between individual businesses and our society as a whole. Thus the operation of our economic system — entrusted to management — demands far more than technical competence in the various functions of business.

At the same time, I would not have you think for a minute that in the last ten years we have lessened our interest in business functions and institutions. In Marketing, Production, Accounting and Statistics, and in Finance we have also moved forward in a development which could well be the subject of another full-length report to you. We are now even more than ever concerned about the essentials of profitable business operations, for no fulfillment of responsibility is possible without profit and continuous success in competition. Research in business methods will and must move forward to maintain this School's identification with the tough business problems which have always constituted our curriculum.

We have not changed our purposes; we have added to them. We ask students to carry not a different but a heavier burden. Administration, as we now conceive it at the School, is a task for tough-minded and mature men who are humble but not timid in the face of their assignment.

I have tried to explain how our ideas of administration have enlarged in recent years. But just as important as where we have been is where we are going. Where will this developing tradition take us? I should like to outline what I conceive to be our goal for the future and the work we still have to do to bring it in sight.

My own pride in the work of this School does not keep me from saying that we still have a very great deal to do in the years ahead. As these concepts of administration are clarified by a pedestrian examination of experience, we can look forward to a series of accomplishments in two areas:

1. Now that we recognize the need to provide for the growth of the individual in a business organization, we must learn more about how to foster that growth and how to reconcile the varieties of individual capacity with the necessity, for example, of achieving particular group objectives in a heavily competitive society. Recognizing the interdependence of all men and nations, we must know more about reconciling the needs of individuals with the larger needs of the groups to which they belong. In the area of human relations, in short, we look forward to discovering ways and means of discharging the obligations inherent in our present idea of administration.

2. In the area of our political and social responsibilities, we need to clarify further the scope of a businessman's responsibilities to what could be an almost infinite number of community claims. We need to know more about how these responsibilities can be efficiently and humanely discharged. In the area of our human and social commitments, we must find out how to merge their fulfillment with the no small task of achieving competitive efficiency. If, as I suspect, attention to these responsibilities will make easier the achievement of efficiency, we must demonstrate this interrelationship. We know that the objectives of business success and social responsibility are by no means in conflict, but we have not yet closed the gap of inexperience that lies between them. No formulas or sets of principles will ever be available as short-cut solutions, but we must hammer out useful ways of thinking about business problems in their human and social context.

As an example of what we must do in the area of social responsibility, we must complete the research necessary for a greater understanding of business, especially big business — yes, and big labor — and for more intelligent and effective governmental regulation of the competitive practices of business and of labor. We should also investigate the role of management in attaining the oft-stated goal of "high-level employment without inflation." Most of the research in this field has dealt with possible monetary and fiscal activities of the government to achieve this goal. We have not yet considered what businessmen can and should do in partnership with government to avoid serious economic fluctuations. Much must be done at the practical level of day-to-day business decisions.

If in the lifetimes of the youngest alumni of the School we are to learn how to *attain* the objectives we can now begin to *see,* we must look upon ourselves, I grow increasingly certain, as a professional school. Not that business can be exactly like the other professions. Administration should not become compartmentalized into specialties, and no professional oath has yet been devised to fit business. But we can have a common set of ideals.

The practice of business administration, through our alumni and those of institutions associated with us, must become professional in performance, in integrity, and in willing acceptance of social obligations. We have clearly made progress in this direction, both in the School and in business. We have made a good start, for example, in such professional activities as the compilation of experience and the recording of data, in developing methods of observation and research, and making available for study thousands of individual situations occurring in business.

We must go much further, however, in the highly professional activity of creating new knowledge, not only by continuing the clinical examination of business situations but by making use of the work of scholars in other fields, particularly the social sciences. It is significant, I think, that our medical schools have adapted to the profession of medicine previously unrelated researches in biology, chemistry, and physics. Soil chemists and microbiologists, for example, have contributed to the prevention and treatment of disease, and students of electricity have advanced both diagnosis and therapy. Great advances in medicine probably still await new applications and combinations of knowledge already in the process of being discovered and tested.

In the area of business and other social activities, experiment is much more difficult. Human affairs do not stand still for microscopic examination. But Dean Donham, Dr. Henderson, and Professor Mayo put together their knowledge of administration, sociology, psychology, and anthropology to produce Human Relations. They had a gift for combination and application much like the medical scientists. These social sciences must contribute much more to our understanding of administration if we are to make progress in the large questions I have already mentioned, like the relationship of the individual to the group and the balancing of individual growth and group accomplishment. The relationship of the medical school to the physical and biological sciences may well be paralleled by the relationship of the business school to the social sciences.

Just as Human Relations cannot move forward apart from the development of knowledge in social science, so our work in the relationships of business to our society requires new combinations of knowledge and concepts developed by political scientists, economists, and scholars of the law. The work of adaptation, as in medicine, is not easy, since the knowledge developed by the social scientists is not always immediately useful. The traditional gap between economics as a social science and business administration is the best known example of this difficulty. We do not yet have, and have not yet developed ourselves (as we must), an economic theory which is a realistic account of business behavior and business competition. This cannot be done merely with the use of statistical aggregates.

But though we do not often find ready-made the knowledge we need, I am convinced that our professional knowledge will move forward together with that of the social sciences. When their work does not apply, we must fill the need ourselves.

But in my hope that we may make professional use of all that is discovered in social studies, I am moved to say that the developing concepts of administration require us to apply to the accomplishment of the world's work the achievements also in the humanities, principally history, religion, literature, music, and art. We know the ways in which these fields contribute to an individual's development.

If administration is to be a profession, administrators, like all other professional men, must have developed breadth of view. Their experience with the humanities should be well advanced before they come to a professional graduate school. A liberal education can, of course, be achieved by other than formal training, just as the professional ranks of management are open to qualified men from other schools or no school at all. There is here, I should say, no monopoly in management.

We also need the knowledge made available by scholarship in these fields. Consider the role of social history, for example. How can we understand the relationship of business to our society without being acquainted with the forces at work in our civilization? How can we move forward in Human Relations to make work a way of life if we are not familiar with the movement and direction of our time? How can we manage a business as a community of people in whom we are genuinely interested without knowing and sharing the goals of our culture? We cannot really know where we are until we know something of where we have been, and we have not yet fully utilized much of what history has to say about where we yet may go and how we might get there.

The literature of our own country, as another example, tells us much about our history and more about the people in whom today we claim a great interest. Philosophy and religion provide the means for giving order to life and make available the Christian ethic as the standard for its conduct. Music and art provide a means for participation in community life, and, as you know, the support of arts by businessmen is a characteristic of our civilization. If our aim in business is a better life, we need to have at hand both the knowledge and the pleasures made available to us by the arts.

As a professional school in a university located in one of the country's oldest cultural centers, it would be wasteful of us in particular to ignore the resources so close at hand.

I have said that I think developing concepts of administration will compel us to become more and more explicitly a professional school. I should like to conclude by referring to another corollary of our forthcoming professional status — the opportunity to *recapture* a set of values which conceives for business administration objectives beyond the creation and maintenance of material wealth. I take it that a profession is marked by the dedication of its members to the goals of the profession. The goal of professional administration, I should like to suggest, is the achievement through our economic system of a full life — beginning but not ending with material plenty.

The direction in which we are moving compels me to say, in all realism, that administration will some day be recognized as the process of conducting business affairs in the interest of a life worth living according to the values of our society and the capacity of each individual. There is, then, for the School and for those in business an opportunity which is spiritual as well as material. We are not only confronted by the challenge to maintain a stable economy; we are also challenged to use it as a means to the kind of life in which men may live in freedom, in peace, and in fulfillment of their spiritual needs.

And we must make the objectives of American business *clear*—for our own guidance and for the enlistment of support from other sections of the world community. That the objectives of business administration are capable of becoming professional in character is not known to the world. The world, indeed, looks distrustfully upon our business civilization as exclusively material.

One of the important problems facing us all today takes the form of a paradox. In that portion of the world dominated by the most materialistic creed in human history — the area behind the iron curtain — the ideology in terms of complete devotion to a cause is essentially like a religion. In the Western World, whose philosophy is spiritual in origin and whose freedom is a magnificent cause, for all men the outlook of life, society, and progress is mostly expressed in quantitative terms. We are said to think in terms of wealth, of material things.

The School, along with business itself, can contribute to the resolution of this paradox. In our work we can contribute to a regeneration of the spiritual values implicit in our professional activities. By the way we live and put into practice the evolving concepts of administration I have described today, I think we can develop a program that will command the devotion of free people and make doing of the world's work a creative achievement. When the things that people do have a clear meaning bound up with their whole lives, they will do those things with an ability and a spirit which will make short work of many of the present-day obstacles to productiveness.

If my looking forward to the time when administration is fully professional seems visionary, then I have not made myself clear. The practicality of our becoming a professional school is implicit in the work already under way. Moving forward is only a common-sense response to the needs of our time. The goals I have described may seem distant. In a sense they are. All sensible objectives are beyond immediate reach; we hitch our wagon to a star.

At the same time, these long-range developments present an immediate challenge to today's business leaders. The training of young men for business is slow. The results are far off. Our new graduates are prepared only to learn well. They still have far to go before they qualify themselves for broad leadership. But today's business leaders are at the point of action. They do not need to wait for us to advance knowledge of human relations and business responsibilities. They can move immediately toward professional ideals day by day.

They can experience for themselves the satisfactions of helping the people within their influence move forward in ability and in maturity. They can experiment with problems of community service. And they can learn the permanence of the nonmaterial rewards of business.

At the very least they have this opportunity — the opportunity to raise the practice of administration toward the levels of competence and of responsibility which the world requires of us. The alteration of our way of life that American businessmen have within their grasp is to me the most exciting aspect of this challenging moment of history.

PART II

HUMAN RELATIONS AND THE MOTIVATION OF PEOPLE

George F. F. Lombard, Abraham Zaleznik, Paul R. Lawrence, and Harriet Ronken

The remarks of the four responsible for this chapter will be focused on some of our more recent experiences in research. This means that we shall not be presenting definite answers, but rather some new directions in which we are beginning to explore, some observations about human behavior the implications of which we find perplexing. We shall do this by presenting to you instances of the ways in which we have observed that problems of human relations and motivation arise in business organizations. We shall tell you not only how we saw some specific individuals behave, but also something about what they themselves thought of their behavior and what it was that they felt they were doing. In this way we shall try to indicate some of the conclusions to which our research is leading us.

We often find ourselves perplexed and confused about the significance of what we are observing. Some of our conclusions tend to contradict many so-called common-sense interpretations of experience. To illustrate what I mean by these "common-sense interpretations of experience," I should like to call your attention to several cartoons which appeared in the Spring 1952 issue of the *Harvard Business School Bulletin*.

We have first the executive who assumes that motivation is concerned with his shoveling things out to people. What he is shoveling are dollars, but I am less concerned with that — for the point I am

NOTE: Mr. Lombard is Associate Professor of Human Relations, Mr. Zaleznik and Mr. Lawrence are Assistant Professors of Business Administration, and Miss Ronken is Associate in Human Relations, Harvard Business School.

The introductory and concluding remarks are by Mr. Lombard; the three case presentations by Mr. Zaleznik, Mr. Lawrence, and Miss Ronken, in that order.

making, they might equally well be pesos, rupees, or bananas — than with his behavior, that it is he who is doing the shoveling.

The executive who pictures himself as shoveling things out of course feels good about what he is doing. He thinks of himself as

generous and kind. He works hard. His motivation is high. Look at the expression on his face. The feelings of the recipients of his largess are by no means as clear. They may not like to find themselves treated as the recipients of largess, particularly when they feel that they have worked long and hard to accumulate these rewards. Maybe that is why the artist decided to leave them out. In doing so,

I think he has accurately portrayed the feelings of people who are being motivated in these ways: they feel left out.

The second cartoon of course is very familiar: "The big stick; it gets results." Here the artist has caught well not only a common idea about motivation, but also the feelings of the people concerned. Notice the expression of concern and fear on the faces of even these on-lookers. Notice also the face of the man who has the club. He is scowling, worried, anxious, or angry. Notice too that the recipients of his anger are left out of the picture. That is characteristic, is it not, of this way of motivating people also? We assume that dollars and the big stick are so useful that one does not have to be particularly discriminating as to how one uses them. The only suggestion we have here is that the executive is angry about something on a piece of paper, else why the brief case in the other hand? This is a rather extraordinary commentary on the behavior of executives — that whoever is to be hit with the club is not there, but the brief case, surely stuffed with papers, is.

At this point I could say much more, but the idea is this: the executive who thinks of himself as getting others to do things for him sometimes ends up with the others not wanting to do these things. This of course presents a problem for the executive, no less than for the person motivated. In our studies we have focused on these problems as they arise in the face-to-face activities and interactions of people. Although these aspects of a situation are of course only a small part of the total environment in which any of us live and work, I think we would all recognize that they are an important part. The physical and economic conditions of work — the paint, the light, the heat, the machines, the wage and salary scales, and the bonus plans — may all be of the finest, but if I do not also like my associates at work and if I cannot speak freely to my boss, my feelings about doing things for him are apt at best to be mixed. The company's organization, its policies and procedures, its employee magazines, its plant bulletin boards, its suggestion systems, all may be excellent, but I still will not be happy if these other matters are not also satisfactory.

In our studies we try to examine the interactions of persons thoroughly. We have of course no such highly perfected tool as a microscope, but we do have the methods of observation and interview. We observe to see who sees whom, how often, and about what. We listen to find out how the persons we are studying perceive and feel about their own and others' behavior. We find that the most difficult part of our task is to understand how another person views the world around him. Much of what we do is addressed to this purpose, for without such understanding what we observe often does not make sense.

But now let us get down to cases.

Case No. 1 — Tony

One of the key persons in the management group upon whom we depend for results is the foreman—the fellow who is supposed to get the goods out. He is on the firing line; and, as he is well aware, the results of his efforts are measured in terms of so many units produced above or below standard. Fortunately, or unfortunately if you happen to be a foreman, somebody is always able to count how many units the work group produced. The problem of motivation for the foreman in his setting is no longer an academic matter. It is wrapped up in his concrete behavior and in the results of his behavior in creating a free and spontaneous desire in people to work toward a common purpose.

I'm going to describe a situation in which this spontaneous desire to help was missing. This story is about a foreman — an "honest-to-goodness" foreman — whose name was Tony. I should like to invite the reader into Tony's hectic world so that together perhaps we can identify what was missing in his and other people's behavior.

Tony wanted desperately to make good on his job, and he approached it with a lot of enthusiasm. But he ran into trouble and was never able to get out of it. His trouble, superficially, had to do with an assembly line. The line was set up carefully by methods engineers so that it was supposed to run continuously and smoothly, with each operator working according to timed jobs. Instead of running the way it was supposed to, however, this automatic gadget did just the opposite. The girls on the assembly line could not keep up with the conveyer; they had to follow the work, chasing other girls out of position, and the solution resorted to only as a measure of desperation was to start and stop the conveyer.

Now I said that Tony's problem was the assembly line, and I called this diagnosis superficial. Actually his problem was people — they did not act the way he expected them to.

Let us look at the situation on this assembly line. Tony was the foreman. His boss was Dan. Working with Tony were three group leaders — Dottie, Helen, and Jean. Under the group leaders were workers — approximately 12 or 13 to each. The conveyer was 480 feet long, but only half of it was being used for production; the other half was for possible expansion. This work arrangement is typical of almost any mass-production setup at the work level.

There were a lot of specialists on the line. The first was a man by the name of Dick, who was head of quality control. Rita was under his supervision, and there were three inspectors working for her and watching for rejects. Bob was another specialist connected with the line. He was a methods man whose job was to set the line up and determine what the work cycle ought to be. He introduced production changes and revisions, and he had a boss whose name was Fred.

Every one of these people had a job to do which was vital to the successful operation of Tony's line. However, most of the people involved, including Tony, seemed to see their jobs as getting something done "come hell or high water," which they interpreted as meaning getting the job done despite the other people in the situation. A specific incident will give us a clearer picture of what was happening on the line.

Tony was getting fed up with the chronic failure of the girls to keep up with the conveyer. So he got a stop watch and began to time a section of the line to find out who was the villain of the piece. Magically, while he was timing the operators, the line ran fairly smoothly. He then turned the watch over to the section's group leader, Helen, and instructed her to keep timing. He left the line and came back a short while later. When he returned, he found to his horror that the girls were far out of position and many units behind, and that in following the work as the conveyer was moving his girls had pushed the quality-control inspectors out of position.

Tony turned to Helen and said, "Helen, the girls were in position while I was watching them. As soon as I left, they got out again. Now what happened?"

Helen: "I don't know, Tony. It's not their fault. Maybe it's the girls up ahead of them."

Tony: "I can't understand, Helen, why this happened. The girls were in position fine, and I go away for a few minutes and come back and find them out of position. Now, how did that happen?"

Helen kept repeating that she thought it was the fault of the girls preceding her section of the line. Tony kept muttering, "I don't understand why that happened."

The line was far out of position when Tony was called by quality-control inspector No. 3. She said, "Look at where I'm working, Tony. I'm way out of position. I should be down there," and she pointed to her place five or six positions from where she was then working.

Quality inspector No. 2 joined in. "Tony, you'll have to stop the conveyer and give us a chance to get back in position."

Tony: "I can't stop the conveyer. We're behind schedule as it is. Now, why should you be so far out of position?"

Jean had an explanation. "Our regular man who puts in the motor is out today. It's a tough position, and we've got an inexperienced man there."

Tony: "Well, we can't stop the conveyer. I lose too much production that way."

The second quality inspector: "Well, we're being pushed out of position. Where will we go?"

And they continued arguing in this vein for some time.

Let us analyze that scene for a moment. We have observed some behavior between a foreman and his subordinates. Almost implicit in Tony's behavior was the need to find someone to blame for the problem. With his approach of "Why did that happen?" and "I can't understand," Tony did not get any help from Helen, one of his group leaders. It is interesting, too, to observe that when Tony did get an explanation from Jean (i.e., that one of her experienced operators was out), Tony appeared not to hear it. He acted on the basis of his immediate concern that stopping the conveyer would result in lost production.

After the quality-control inspectors continued to complain that they were being pushed out of position, Tony took some action. He called for one of the repair men and told him to take some units off the line. Tony himself took one unit off the conveyer and placed it on the floor. Just then his boss, Dan, came by.

Dan: "What's that unit doing on the floor?"

Tony: "I just took it off the line."

Dan: "Well, look, get it off the floor right away, and I don't want to ever see a unit on the floor again. Get me?"

This bawling out from his boss, who did not appear interested in why Tony took a unit off the line or in the difficulties Tony was experiencing, must have generated some feelings of anger, helplessness, and guilt in Tony. He continued his heated argument with the quality-control inspectors, and in doing so projected some of these feelings on to the people below him. They urged him to stop the conveyer, but he steadfastly refused.

At this point Rita and her boss, Dick, came hurrying down the aisle. They were immediately joined by Bob, the methods man.

Dick: "Look, Tony, I want these units taken out of my inspectors' positions right away. Look at where they are. They've been pushed out of their positions. They can't move the lights [special fluorescents installed over their work positions] any further. I'm not going to have my inspectors work in the dark. Now get those units out of their positions."

Tony: "Now wait a minute, Dick. I'm doing the best I can. I already have five units moved from the line. What more do you want me to do?"

Dick: "I don't care what you do. Just have those units out of the way. It's not my fault your girls can't keep up with the line."

Tony: "Aw, now listen, Dick, don't say that. They're keeping up."

Dick: "What do you call 'keeping up'? Look for yourself. Your last girl is right in my inspector's position. Look at that."

Tony: "Now look, Dick, I have somebody out this morning. That's what's holding the line up."

Dick: "I don't care about that. It's your responsibility to take care of those things. But I shouldn't be penalized for it."

Tony: "Dick, don't say that! Who's penalizing you? I'm doing what I can to get this straightened out. I'm trying to get methods over here to move my last position and then to move your inspectors down. I saw Fred and Dan, but I don't get any satisfaction out of them. I've been after Fred for a week to get it done, but nothing happens."

Bob: "Just a minute here. I heard about moving your last position only last night. What am I supposed to do? I just heard about it, and you expect me to have it done already."

Tony said, "I sent Fred a memo last week, and nothing's been done yet."

Bob: "Well, you didn't tell me. I just heard about it last night."

Tony: "I'm saying I told Fred."

Bob: "How did you tell him?"

Tony: "I said I sent Fred a memo."

Bob: "Well, I didn't hear anything until last night."

Dick: "Look, this doesn't help me any. I want those units moved out of my inspectors' positions. It's not my fault your line can't keep up."

Tony: "Stop saying that. I've been checking my line all morning, and they're keeping up."

Bob: "Keeping up! Well, what do you call this?"

Dick: "Look at where your people are now."

Bob: "And it was that way last night, too."

Tony: "Not just last night. Look, it's been that way for a week."

Bob: "Well, that makes it even worse."

Tony: "Yeah, but I've been after methods to move my last position for a week."

Bob: "Well, I'm telling you I just heard about it last night."

Dick: "Look, Tony, are you interested in having inspection?"

Tony: "Certainly I am, Dick."

Dick: "Well, you certainly don't act that way. My girls will have to work in the dark, and I'm not going to stand for that. You're not coöperating with me."

Tony: "Look, don't say I'm not coöperating with you."

Dick: "Well, what else can I think?"

Bob: "The line being out of position has nothing to do with methods."

Rita: "Now wait a minute. I know that Tony is bending over backward to help me. The last position should have been moved long ago."

Bob: "What do you know about this, Rita? What are you talking for?"

Rita: "I know plenty, but I haven't got as big a mouth as some people, so I don't talk."

Bob: "If you're referring to me, Rita, it looks like you're looking for an argument. And that's the first time anyone's heard you wanting to keep quiet."

Tony: "Sure, Rita knows. Haven't I been working on this?"

Rita nodded, but Dick said, "Look, this is getting us nowhere fast. I want those units moved, and I'm going to get someone who'll see that they are moved." He started to walk away saying, "All these supervisors care about is getting production. They don't give a damn about quality, but I'm not going to let them get away with that."

In the above interaction, conflict between the foreman and the staff specialists is the primary theme. From Tony's point of view, Dick was accusing him of not coöperating, of not wanting to turn out a product with good quality and, implied in all this, of being incompetent. What Tony heard in Bob's remarks was that Bob refused to accept responsibility for the line's problems or, turned the other way, that Tony was completely at fault in the situation. In the little byplay between Bob and Rita, which only added confusion to the scene, they were expressing hostile feelings toward one another. In the midst of all this, it is especially interesting to note that no one was diagnosing the problems of the line. The conflict reached the point where Tony was not even able to observe and accept what was apparent to others — that the line was not keeping up. He was reacting so completely to the threat which he perceived in Dick's behavior that he literally could not see the condition of the line.

In the final scene in this incident, we again have the chance to look at the relationship between Tony and his boss, Dan. Dick had left to go after Dan. Tony then stopped the conveyer. In a minute or two, Dick returned with Dan. Here's what happened:

Dan: "Tony, come over here. Stop the line. Look, you're going to have to keep from interfering with Dick's girls."

Tony: "Dan, I'm not interfering with Dick's girls."

Dan: "Well, look over there. What do you call this? Now stop the conveyer."

Tony: "I have. But I've been working on why the girls have been getting out of position all morning."

Dan: "Look, Tony, they're out of position now, aren't they? Answer me that."

Tony: "Yes."

Dan: "They're over in Dick's girls' positions, aren't they? Answer me that."

Tony: "Yes."

Dan: "You're the supervisor here, aren't you? Well, you're responsible for it, so get your people out of the way of Dick's girls. Now stop the conveyer!"

Tony: "I have."
Dan: "Okay."

For Tony, this interaction with his boss was almost the last straw. Here he had been trying to keep the conveyer running to get output, which was what his boss wanted. Dan, however, was ordering him to stop the conveyer. On top of this, Dan was letting him know very plainly that he alone was responsible for the chaotic conditions on the line. Notice again that Dan was so preoccupied with "telling Tony off" that he did not even see or hear that Tony had already stopped the conveyer.

Now, as you can imagine, Tony was feeling very depressed as a result of the incident which I have described. Here is what he said to me:

"You heard what they said. I'm glad you listened and heard it all. I've been after methods for a week to move the last position, and I couldn't get anything done. I see Dan and Fred, and I don't get any satisfaction. Then they blame me. You heard Dick say I don't coöperate. Well, they always say that whenever they want to end an argument. They tell me I don't coöperate. That isn't right."

He paused for a minute and then went on, "I'm really worried, and I don't know what to do. Dan said to me before that he wants to speed up the conveyer tomorrow. He also told me never to stop the conveyer. What am I supposed to do? He tells me one thing and then turns around and orders me to stop the conveyer. That gets me all confused. Now, I'm not asking you for your opinion, but you heard it all. What was I supposed to do?"

Tony was expressing to me all the feelings of worry, frustration, and fear which his experience had generated in him. He was feeling caught in the middle of a conflict, a conflict between his desires and the behavior of others. He was in the middle between his goal of succeeding on the job, which meant to him getting output, on the one hand, and the aggressive, threatening behavior of his associates (his boss Dan, Dick, and the other staff specialists) and the perplexing characteristics of his line, on the other hand. The conveyer just would not keep running right.

Tony felt very much alone with his problems. No one was offering him any help. People, instead of being sources of help, became blocks. He summarized his feelings about this in a later interview:

> You know something; you see a lot of people who come down to the line and try to tell me what to do. Look at all the people I got to confront with. There's methods; then there's inspection and engineering. And then I got to confront with my boss. That means I got to confront with five different people. And they don't want to know the other side of the story. They only look at their side.

But why do we concentrate on Tony? Wasn't it the responsibility and function of the methods man, Bob, to make sure the assembly line was working properly before it was given to Tony, and to follow it up to iron out possible bottlenecks? Shouldn't that be part of good organization and procedure policy? Of course, it should be. But how do you isolate what is a problem of the assembly line? Operators began to stay out; they were replaced with inexperienced operators. Whose responsibility was that?

It was also very possible that the line was not balanced and therefore would not function properly. But can you look at the problem so simply? Certainly it is curious and very interesting to note that the line was not tested till some time after it was running. That was a simple step; yet it was not taken. Things that seem obvious to us were completely ignored. Why wasn't an attempt made to test it and isolate the difficulty? The answer lies in how individual people were thinking and feeling. The people concerned with the line were wrapped up in their own feelings, and a request on somebody else's part made them feel they were being threatened.

The big question is: How do we help our Tonys, our Dans, and our staff specialists? How do we reverse a pattern of behavior which is vicious — vicious because the job was not getting done and people actually disliked their work environment. Listen to how one operator felt about her job: "God, I hate this place. It's not the work; I like that. But it's the bosses. I never thought work would be like this. You're chained to your position. You can't go to the bathroom or get a drink of water. The bosses are so mean."

It would be simpler and perhaps more comforting to talk about motivations in the abstract, but our experience shows us over and over again that our conclusions about motivation and behavior must make sense in a concrete situation such as I have described.

Do we approach the problem as individuals, each carrying our club to force other people into behaving the way we want them to? Remember, Tony's club was a stop watch, and the results of his wielding it did not last long. Dan's club was much less subtle; but, as later incidents showed, it frightened Tony and did not help him in his relationships with the people on his assembly line.

On Tony's assembly line there was a conspicuous lack of the spontaneous desire on the part of people to help get things done. To my way of thinking, this spontaneous coöperation failed to develop because several important ingredients were missing in the behavior of all the key people with administrative responsibility. First, no one was stopping to understand the situation, a large part of which included the feelings and needs of the people on the job. Secondly, no one was acting in a way which indicated that he was interested in the difficulties as others perceived them. And, finally, no one seemed to be aware of the effects of his behavior on the feelings and behavior of others. This last missing element is extremely important. Awareness of the effects of our behavior on others is a powerful skill and a first step toward changing behavior.

The question still remains: How do you develop people who are in positions of administrative responsibility so that they become self-aware? Formal training — the kind where supervisors are brought together as a group and given an opportunity to reflect on their own experience — has received considerable attention of late, and it provides a great opportunity. But it will not work if it verges on classroom lecturing; it is a slow process at best; and in Tony's case it may not work anyway until other things are changed. The way things are, he may see formal training as another pressure. First somebody must give an indication that he understands Tony.

Actually there is no *one* way to train Tony; there are a lot of ways, most of them informal. If somebody — his boss, or one of the staff specialists, or even a subordinate — just acts differently in approaching the problem, then the desired change in Tony may begin;

Tony may begin to look around and search a little bit and see things in a new way. So maybe the best way to train Tony to feel and act differently is to train Dan, his boss.

Case No. 2 — Jim

We have discussed a dramatic episode involving Tony, the foreman, what happened to him, and how he reacted. Here was a foreman in action. Now let us consider a foreman doing something different — namely, thinking out loud about his job situation.

At the time of this interview, Jim had only recently been reassigned to a new job and given a new boss. He started talking to the interviewer about a very common topic — money — and then went on to talk about some other matters that were important to him. The conversation ran something like this:

Jim: "Well, suppose you are working — not getting enough money, but as much as possible. Your boss understands you and you've worked there for a long time. Things are man-to-man. And then you get a different job, and things aren't the same any more. You think you're doing all right on the new job, but you don't know. Maybe they can hire a better man, maybe not. You start working harder on things that will be noticed — things you know the boss is watching, but not some other things you might be doing. Suppose you're getting $300 a month. You look around and where could you get more money?"

Interviewer: "You want to do a good job, but things aren't right?"

Jim: "Yes, because it's on an 'or else' basis. It's different if a man is used to quitting a job; if he doesn't have a family. But you don't feel you can let your wife down. What you have to do to keep your job!"

Interviewer: "You mean you're only getting money?"

Jim: "No, that's not true. Well, maybe it is. Why, I used to wait for Monday morning. A holiday was all right, but I kept looking forward to what I was going to do on Monday. That's funny, but I'm talking the way I feel. Now, my boss makes you efficiency conscious. It's not that you like the job these days — it's just dollars and cents."

Interviewer: "Something is missing and it bothers you?"

Jim: "Yes, there's no responsibility. But they can only let you have responsibility if they're sure themselves. If they're not sure of themselves, you can't be either and it affects your work. You just do the things that they will notice, and what you think they want you to do. Hell, it's part of my work to make decisions. Sure, I make them. I have to all the time. But only when I know I'm right and not on anything that could possibly go wrong. And the trouble is that if you went ahead, you'd probably be right anyway."

Interviewer: "You mean, Jim, you can't do the job the way you want to?"

Jim: "Yes, you're afraid to try. Oh, I know that you can't go ahead on everything — not on something big. But on most things, if they gave you a chance to go ahead and think it over for a while, you'd come up with an idea that wouldn't be too far wrong. Remember those jigs I used to make? Only a small job. Maybe that's the best I could do. Maybe it was crude, but it got the job done. Maybe it was as good as anybody could do anyway."

Interviewer: "But you feel you're not going that far now?"

Jim: "That's right. You know you can do things they don't know you can do. If all a man can do is dig ditches, he knows. I can do a lot of things in my own field, and I know what I can't do, too. But they're not letting me do as much as I could. I only go so far, and then I let somebody else do the job — make decisions I could make."

Interviewer: "Then you feel it's up to them to give you the chance to make these decisions?"

Jim: "Sure, it's up to them to give you the rope. Sure, you might make mistakes; everybody does. This way you don't make them, but you don't do things you could do either. I'm talking about somebody who is serious about his work and knows what he's doing. If he's been given a chance, he'll get everything out that's humanly possible. There aren't many men who don't care about how they do a job."

Interviewer: "Yet your hands are tied?"

Jim: "Yes, there are many people who can do a good job, who want to, and yet people won't let them. Hell, I guess I'm doing it myself with the guys working for me. It works all the way down the line. I don't let them do things unless I'm absolutely sure that they can do them, because I'm afraid of what will happen if they make mistakes. I don't get the best out of my men, and my bosses don't get the best out of me. It's the same all down the line."

Interviewer: "It's all a vicious circle?"

Jim: "That's human nature, isn't it? Somebody on top is afraid of human error. You don't get a chance to do your best and then explain what happened."

Interviewer: "And there's no way out?"

Jim: "How are you going to do it? They're just not getting enough out of me now. Before I wanted to do it. All my old boss had to say was, 'It's important to me,' and I broke my back to do it. That meant an awful lot to me — more than my pay."

Interviewer: "And you don't want to do it any more?"

Jim: "I don't think so now. I'm working now only because of my pay and because, if I don't, they'll get somebody else who will. You know, you don't think about doing as little as you can when things are going well and you're happy. Hell, the people who aren't happy are the only ones worrying about getting more pay. If you're happy, you don't even think about your pay until payday, and then, of course, you find you haven't got enough money to pay your bills. The less you like to work, the more you want to get paid because you haven't got anything else to think about. If you like your job, it excites your imagination. It's natural to work your head off — to do things you're not asked to do — things that aren't an issue. But if you can't get excited about it, you just don't feel like it."

In this conversation Jim is expressing feelings that to some degree we have all had at one time or another. I don't think there is anything unusual about Jim's feelings. However, when we are the bosses that deal with the Jims, we often tend to forget these matters. You see, in order for Jim to do a better job he doesn't need more pressure or pushing from his boss; he doesn't need more demands, more checking up. What he does need, though, is his boss's confidence, and freedom — freedom from the fear of making mistakes, freedom from the fear of going "all out" on his job, freedom to take responsibility and do the job in the very best way he can. Jim does not have to be made to do his work to enjoy it; he wants to get a kick out of working hard and making a real and recognized contribution. The problem for Jim's boss is not how to motivate Jim to work, but how to set the conditions that release Jim's innate desire to do a job.

With the benefit of this interview we can understand Jim, but I wonder how his boss looks at him. He might well see Jim as a rather slow, cautious, inexperienced man who needs a lot of urging, detailed instructions, and checking up to see that he is doing the job exactly the way the boss wants so that the higher-ups will stay off his neck. What would have happened if Jim could have said directly to his boss what he told the interviewer? I am sure Jim's boss would have learned some things that would have helped the situation. If he really understood Jim's feelings, he could not help but change his appraisal of Jim and begin to treat Jim differently.

But the fact remains that it was an interviewer, not the boss, who learned these things about Jim. What was the interviewer's magic that allowed him to get to understand Jim so well? No magic at all — the interviewer was simply interested in listening carefully to Jim and learning from him the things that were important to him. It was that simple. This, of course, is very hard to do if you are the boss with a lot of worries and a lot of things you want to get out of Jim. We can see, though, that if it could have been done, it would have paid off. Not only would the boss have learned something from Jim, but the miracle is that Jim would have learned something also. As it was, Jim said, "Hell, I guess I'm doing it with the people working for me." Here Jim suddenly realized that he was doing to his own men the same thing his boss was doing to him. I am pretty sure this is the first time Jim realized this, and it was a significant step for Jim to take.

Of course, you can point out rightly that Jim has not as yet used this realization in his dealings with his own men. However, we have seen in our studies time and again that this kind of insight and new awareness of a situation is the first step toward more constructive behavior. Tony, the foreman in the first case, did not realize what was happening to him. Jim, the foreman in this case, has gone a step further in his realization and awareness of what his actions are doing to his own subordinates. It is a promising step in the right direction. The interviewer has simply helped in this process. And any one of us can help like this if we can learn to understand our own subordinates in the way that this interviewer understood Jim.

Still at the end of the interview Jim feels somewhat trapped and uncertain as to what he can do about his situation. He is posing a dilemma that many of our supervisors in industry face, namely, how can they live with a sense of uncertainty in their relations with their own bosses and still develop a constructive and healthy atmosphere for their own subordinates? The next case provides some material that may give us a lead, at least to the extent that it describes one man's solution to the same kind of dilemma.

Case No. 3 — Ben

So far we have discussed some rather common assumptions regarding what makes people work and, even more to the point, work *together*. We have seen one little piece of behavior — a short extract from life — in which Tony and some other supervisors were acting on the basis of those assumptions. Next we have heard another foreman, Jim, doing what almost amounted to thinking out loud; he was raising questions about those assumptions, and his questions were based on his own feelings about the treatment he himself had received. In this final case we are going to hear from a foreman who ultimately came to have a different point of view.

After a few pretty troublesome years this foreman had worked through to a quite different set of implicit assumptions about the motivations of the people who worked for him. Far from assuming that it was up to him to light fires under his subordinates, he assumed that they came equipped with self-starters which would function so long as he did not mess up the works, so long as he did not prevent their own motives from functioning. He recognized that motivations might be different for different people, or for the same people at different times; it was not, therefore, a matter of some one thing, however complex, that he could provide for his workers, but rather it was a matter of what they brought with them to the work situation. He also assumed that once he had trained his subordinates in their jobs, they were adequate to the ordinary course of events. He believed that his workers wanted to do a good job unless he, by his behavior, made them not want to.

In order to make more understandable the situation involving this foreman and the way he came to these assumptions, I should like to fill in a little background for you. The foreman was a young man whom I shall call Ben. Several years ago Ben was assigned to organize and supervise a department which would manufacture a new product. The department consisted of 20 women who performed a complex operation, each working at her own speed at her individual machine. At first, until the bugs were ironed out of the new process, the operators were not able to maintain any consistent volume of output. Sometimes they made 25 acceptable units in an hour, and sometimes as few as 5. When the major problems had been straightened out, however, production leveled off at around 35 units an hour.

About a year later the company began a program of expansion. Ben was transferred to a new plant, to set up a second group which would manufacture the same product. To help him train the 20 new operators and "get production rolling" Ben took with him two operators from his original group. At the same time, certain changes in methods and equipment made possible a significant rise in worker productivity, which was expressed by a production standard of 67 units an hour, almost double the previous one. This was considered a good standard — not a tight one. But the new department did not meet it.

Even after Ben had trained the new girls and allowed a reasonable time for them to work up speed, he found that they consistently produced an average of about 35 units, and he could not get output above that point. Eventually he learned that one of the experienced operators had been telling the new girls not to go over 35. Although he had taught her the new methods and explained the new standard to her, she still said to the other girls that 35 had been the standard at the old location, and that if they showed they could crack the new standard, it would again be raised.

Shortly after Ben learned of this fact, the girl who had insisted on the lower output went out on a month's leave. Ben tried to take advantage of her absence to raise output, but his efforts were not very successful. Then one day an incident happened which is best told in Ben's own words:

I haven't had such good relations with the main office since I came out here. In fact, we've had about 12 fights. Well, sometimes I get pretty upset. I slam down the receiver of the telephone in my office, and I go out there to the line and I pace up and down the aisle, and I'm keeping my eye on what's happening to the product, and I don't even see the people. They say something to me, and I don't even hear it; I just ignore them.

Well, a couple of weeks ago I realized what I was doing. You see, what had happened was that we needed some new jigs. An awful lot of those jigs have been used since we first started. They are getting pretty worn; they don't hold things in very tight alignment. The girls have to make allowances for that. They ought to have some new equipment, and management promised it to us.

Well, when the office gave me a date on it, I believed it. I thought this would raise the girls' morale a little bit, give them something to look forward to; so I said to them that next week they were going to get some new equipment. Then my boss called and said, "It won't be out next week; it will be another week!" So I had to tell the girls that my first date was wrong, and they would have to wait another week. By the time that goes on a couple of times, pretty soon the girls stop having confidence in me.

Well, then my boss called and said that we couldn't have the equipment, that it wasn't coming at all; that is, it would come after a while, but he didn't know when. That was pretty disappointing. I had to tell the girls that it wouldn't even be next week, and I couldn't tell them when it would be. So I started thinking about this, and I called them together and had a little talk with them.

I told them that the equipment wasn't coming; I thought they deserved it, but there wasn't anything that could be done about getting it for them under the circumstances. I said I knew they would be disappointed, and that I was disappointed, too. In fact, I told them that I had been disappointed pretty often lately, and I knew I'd been taking it out on them. But I didn't see any reason why I should kick them just because I felt kicked around by my boss. I said I thought we had a good group, that they were a good bunch of kids. There was a lot we could do together; we could have a big, happy family and get a lot done on our own. So I said, "Let's start over again. We can have a good time among ourselves and do the best we can and be friends regardless of what happens in the main office!"

Very shortly after this incident, the group began to reach the output standard of 67 units an hour. When the senior operator returned, she saw that the volume averaged close to standard. For her part, she not only produced 67 an hour, but one hour she even made 81 units.

This is undoubtedly an oversimplification of the events; there were other factors which also contributed to the sudden rise in production. But we have here some of the critical factors. These facts might be interpreted in a great variety of ways. Some supervisors might consider that Ben had gone "soft-headed," while to others it might look as though he had "got religion." My interpretation is different.

First of all we have Ben. Ben was a foreman, the man in the middle. Two or three years ago he was given a brand-new line, manufacturing a newly designed product. The unit was an improved subassembly which went into a number of the company's products. In effect, management had told Ben that there were many bugs still to be ironed out; but that when he got production rolling, he would be top dog in a big, important department. About the time Ben got his department to that state, however, management changed its mind. Instead of a single large department manufacturing this product, there were to be small departments producing the subassembly in each of the plants where it was to be used. This changed the picture for Ben; once he got one line rolling, he had to give it up and go through the same thing with a second small line.

Here he was remote from his boss, and he received information and instructions only over the telephone or through routine reports. This contact was not too satisfactory, and it tended to be brief and terse. Even more important than that, Ben was not in contact with his supervisor's thinking as a process but saw only the end results. In their brief exchanges on the telephone or through the mail, tentative decisions often looked final, suggestions looked like orders, progress reports were indistinguishable from commitments. So it began to seem to Ben that his boss did not understand his problems, did not keep his promises, did not back him up, and was not to be relied on. All this produced in Ben very natural feelings of uncertainty, anxiety, and resentment; but those feelings could not be expressed in his contacts up the chain of command.

Consequently, those feelings found expression in Ben's relations with his subordinates, where they were not appropriate and where they badly confused the signals. The operators, for instance, had no way of knowing, when Ben snapped at them on quality, that he was saying, "I have nothing against you; it's my boss I'm mad at." The girls perceived this behavior as communicating, "I don't care about you. All I'm interested in is high-volume, quality production; it doesn't matter how good a job you are doing now, you will have to do better."

Under such circumstances the girls' motivation was not in the direction of doing the "best" job possible. Rather, it was concerned with protecting themselves against the unreasonable demands of a boss who threatened both their personal integrity and their job security. From their point of view, in terms of their motivation, output pegged at a uniform rate was a logical way of achieving their ends. Any attempt on Ben's part to motivate them to higher output only reinforced their conviction of the need to protect themselves as they were doing.

Suddenly, however, Ben realized the extent to which his behavior was influenced by his feelings. He also began to realize how that behavior might be differently perceived by the operators, and how those perceptions, in turn, aroused feelings in the girls. When Ben got his group together for his little talk, it may well have been the recognition of those feelings that was the important thing he accomplished. Translated according to this view, what Ben was saying might have sounded something like this: "I seem to have a lot of feelings about my job. Recognizing them helps me to realize that you must have feelings, too. Let's accept one another as people of integrity and go on from there."

Ben's use of the big stick had made that stick increasingly necessary and increasingly futile. His recognition of the feelings — the things that were making his operators behave as they were — *freed* them and *allowed* them to work toward the organizational objective (the thing that Ben had tried to motivate them to do) without fear and without violating their own integrity.

The remarkable thing about this story is that Ben achieved this insight on his own. Sudden shifts in the level of productivity do occur in industry, probably much oftener than we hear about. Of those which we know, many have occurred in connection with certain sorts of research activities, such as the Hawthorne Western Electric studies. It is true that Ben had at one time had contact with a research project concerned with the human relations in his department, and during that study he gave some evidence of increasing understanding of his role. But the situation described occurred in the normal course of events in his working life. He was in the same situation he had faced the day before, and he was still the target of the same sorts of pressures being exerted on him from all sides.

Still he was able to develop an awareness of the effects of his behavior on other people and, in the light of that awareness, to reevaluate his own behavior. This is to me the dramatic, really significant part of this story. It suggests the tremendous human potential in these organizations. Ben did not get his subordinates to make the standard, but he did learn something about what was involved in not preventing them from doing so.

This was a new orientation for Ben. We have seen only the first step and the possibilities which that opened up for him. But perhaps that is enough to point up the contrast in the assumptions on which Tony and Ben operated, and to show how those different assumptions led to different types of behavior, both by the men and by their subordinates. For Ben, his new orientation helped to free them all to do what Jim had wished he dared do — throw the best of himself into his job. In this case, undoubtedly, *accident* played some part; the change might not have taken place if the senior operator had not happened to leave temporarily. But the point is that some understanding of what our behavior means to the people with whom we come in contact often helps management to create a climate in which coöperation can grow up.

Conclusion

If we were to sum up what we have been saying, we could do no better than to point first to the assumption about motivation underlying the theme of this book, "getting people to do things." The assumption about behavior that underlies this statement is that it is fruitful for an executive to think of people as the means for the achievement of nonpersonal or organizational ends. This is a common assumption about motivation in the world today. It is evident in the statements and behavior of persons in positions of responsibility at all levels of organized activities. But many of us have observed that something frequently happens in connection with the behavior of an executive who acts on this assumption. The persons whom he is supposed to be motivating often do not like what is happening to them. The executive who behaves in this way often ends up with the persons he assumes he has been motivating feeling that they do not want to do what they are being asked to do. That is, the executive has produced exactly the opposite result from what he intended.

Though this is a common experience, all of us also know people for whom others like to do things, even rather extraordinary, difficult, arduous tasks. Our research suggests that, when this happens, the behavior of the executive is not based on the assumption which we have already stated but on a rather different one, namely, that persons have needs that must be satisfied, just as organizations have purposes that must be secured. The administrator assumes that his task is to facilitate both processes, the satisfaction of personal needs as well as the securing of organizational purposes. As we have tried to show, the implications of these assumptions take us a long way from the lessons of so-called common experience.

LABOR RELATIONS: UNION POWER AND TEAMWORK IN AMERICAN INDUSTRY

James J. Healy, Stephen H. Fuller, Ben A. Lindberg, John T. Dunlop, and Benjamin M. Selekman

The subject of union power is an important one because of the rise in union membership from three million persons some twenty years ago to over fifteen million today; yet it is only recently that many persons have made a searching analysis of the impact of unions on our economy

If we examine some of the academic works which have come out in recent years, we find emerging two extreme points of view.

On the one side is the theory that the results of unionization on a broad, powerful scale will be disastrous, that union policies and attitudes are incompatible with the type of free-enterprise system we have and eventually will bring about the collapse of the free-enterprise system. Those who subscribe to this view ordinarily cite at great length the erosion of management rights which has taken place within the past ten years as a result of growing unionization.

On the other hand, we find some academicians taking the point of view that when one considers the original objectives of unions, they represent the growth of an institution which is surprisingly conservative. These analysts of the labor-relations scene invariably

NOTE: Mr. Healy is Assistant Professor of Industrial Relations, Mr. Fuller is Assistant Professor of Business Administration, Mr. Lindberg is Associate Professor of Business Administration, Mr. Selekman is Kirstein Professor of Labor Relations, Harvard Business School; Mr. Dunlop is Public Member, National Wage Stabilization Board, and Professor of Economics and Member of the Faculty of the Graduate School of Public Administration, Harvard University.

After Mr. Healy's introduction, Mr. Fuller discusses the breeding of power concepts in the shop, Mr. Lindberg deals with personnel techniques at the foreman level, Mr. Dunlop analyzes current issues in public policy, and Mr. Selekman develops the idea of conflict and resolution.

draw a contrast between the union movement in the United States and labor movements in the rest of the world which are identified closely with political movements, often of a socialistic stamp.

Obviously, both these extreme views cannot be right. Here, in this chapter, we are concerned with an analysis of which view comes closer to the truth — and the answer lies not in academic theory but in the actual working out of the problem of power versus teamwork. We shall explore this problem first at the plant level and then at the national level.

Power and Teamwork Incompatible

I want to set forth the proposition that *at the plant level* "power" and teamwork are incompatible. (I have in mind the day-to-day relationships between union and management in the shop, not the negotiation of collective-bargaining agreements or the arbitration of points at issue under such agreements.) Administrative philosophy may be based on power, or it may be built around the concept of teamwork — either one or the other; you cannot have both in the same plant at the same time.

Consider the following list of administrative concepts, consisting as it does of actual statements made to me by various individuals in industry at one time or another:

1. A good leader does not let the workers do what they want to. He should make the decisions and give his recommendations and then check up to see that they are being followed.
2. A leader should provide a specific program of action with a deadline.
3. A leader who lacks power and authority, or having power and authority fails to exercise them, is inefficient.
4. A leader must maintain control of his workers and thus maintain respect.
5. No leader can admit a mistake either to subordinates or to superiors without weakening his own power and authority.
6. Giving approval to a subordinate's suggestion constitutes a threat to a superior's position.
7. When people refuse to coöperate, a good leader should put them

in their place by taking a firm attitude toward them. This will convince them of the futility of their absurd stand.

8. By resisting changes, the leader will be able to preserve his status.

These concepts underlie all the day-to-day union-management relations in the shops where the individuals who stated them work. Those individuals conceive of themselves as being superior and all-wise. And they stand ready to impose unilateral decisions on others in their organizations through the *power* of their authoritative positions. Their self-concept and lack of insight add up to the kind of administrative philosophy which is inconsistent with the development of any type of teamwork.

Do not such statements as those above sound typical of many union leaders, shop stewards, or local union presidents? To some perhaps they do. But the fact is that not a single one of those statements came from a union leader or from a union man. Each and every one was made by a business executive. I suggest that many members of management are gravely concerned by the "power-threat" of unions *not* because it is so different from their own philosophy but because it is so similar. In other words, some managements have power concepts which appear to foster similar power concepts in the leadership of unions. The attitudes, sentiments, and beliefs about administration which management holds are just as significant in determining whether power or teamwork will prevail as those which labor holds.

As an example of my theory that management power leads to union power, let us see what actually happened in two different shops. Here is a very brief exchange between a worker named Fred and his foreman, drawn from case research of the Harvard Business School:

Fred: "How about this job here? You can't get anywhere the way the production rate I am supposed to make is fixed now."

Foreman: "This job was set in April. You started only in June."

Fred: "That don't make any difference to me. As it is now, I never do get into the money."

Foreman: "Well, I know this job is set O.K. because I went over the whole thing with the engineer, and it is right . . . What kind of work did you do before you came here anyway?"

Fred: "I worked on a farm."

Foreman: "The job you are working on is set properly. You are just in here from the farm for a few months and you think you are an expert on rate setting now, I suppose."

Fred: "No. I don't pretend to know too much, but I do have a few ideas."

Foreman: "Well, when I want your help, I will come around and ask you. At present, I don't have a farm; I don't own any orange trees. *I'm not like you* . . . Don't get me wrong. If I didn't know all about the facts in this case, then I would do something about it. But with this job it happens that I followed it myself with the engineer . . . I guess it is your tough luck."

This supervisor does not have the ability to recognize that those who work under his direction are affected or influenced by the same motivating factors as he is. Nor can he imagine himself in Fred's place and appreciate how he, himself, would feel under the same or similar circumstances. Quite the contrary. The foreman told the worker, "I'm not like you." Thus the foreman used his *power* as a supervisor to put Fred "in his place."

Today Fred is an enthusiastic union member; but we should not be surprised to learn that Fred consistently encourages irresponsible union behavior. A foreman, in exercising his position of power as a manager, can create "anti-power" in workers, who will be anxious to use the power of their union membership on management, whether it be in the matter of a strike vote, a wildcat stoppage, or a restriction of production.

Let us look at a second example of how management power created union power in the shop and destroyed any hope of teamwork — the story of a girl by the name of Betty, told in her own words:

I asked the supervisor how much production I would be expected to turn in daily, and she secured this information for me. It seemed like a fantastic amount, but she assured me that after a few days I would be really quite efficient.

A few weeks later one of the girls asked me how I was doing. She looked at my production sheet and swore. She was astonished at how much I was producing each hour. She bitterly reminded me that the girls who had been here six months or even years were not producing what I had accomplished in a few weeks. I was immediately severely ostracized.

For the next couple of weeks I got nothing but the silent treatment. The campaign went on exactly as they planned. My production was dropping. The assistant foreman asked me if I was ill. When I told him my troubles, he advised me to see the foreman, Mr. Lipton, which I did.

Mr. Lipton listened, asking me the names of each of the rebels. Then he assured me justice would prevail. But I noticed no change.

My relief came in the form of a temporary transfer to another department. I knew it would take some time before the girls would become acquainted with my case and the silent treatment would begin. I was shocked to find that no one in that new department was interested in my reputation. I was further surprised to notice the amount of coöperation which prevailed in this department. It is my opinion that it was *due to the fact that the boss was a capable, understanding man.*

Then I was told to return to my former department, where I was greeted by my former boss with a smile, "Did you enjoy your vacation?" This struck me as not being very complimentary to one who has been conscientious from the beginning.

Mr. Lipton, the foreman, continued, "I want you to get back to your machine and sit down; mind your own business." This I was told before I had a chance to speak. He said he wanted me to quit complaining . . . I then told him, "I think I am going to leave." He said, "Now that you mention it, perhaps it is for the best."

Once again, a few more concrete facts by way of epilogue: Betty has not left. At the time of the case she was a member of the union; today she is the shop steward in this same company. And since she has become steward, the number of grievances in her department has mounted alarmingly, over 50 per cent of them centering around the issue of work load and the speed of production. Betty has been trained to use the power of union stewardship to checkmate productivity. The teacher was her foreman, Mr. Lipton, who made a "power-conscious" union leader out of her. Betty is dedicated to the use of power and to the sabotage of potential teamwork.

Our choice at the everyday working level is between teamwork and power — and by power I mean both union power and management power. We cannot have teamwork and power together. Moreover the power chain from union to management can best be broken by management — but only by a management whose basic philosophy has developed from one of knowing all the answers and giving all the orders to one which seeks the genuine participation and teamwork of employees and their union representatives.

Personnel Practices Impinging on Union Power and Teamwork

I believe it to be useful today to consider four particular personnel practices as these impinge on the concept of union power and teamwork at the foreman level of the organization: (1) the selection of foremen and supervisors; (2) the training of foremen or first-line supervisors; (3) the organizational status of these same foremen and supervisors; and (4) the concept of promotion from within that is so typically American.

One of the more recent developments in the selection of foremen and supervisors is an increasingly heavy emphasis on formal education, especially in those areas that make for verbal facility. The foreman was always expected to be able to give effective directions and orders about the work to be performed. But now he also is supposed to be a leader. Moreover, he is expected to be a good speaker — one who can hold his audience at a group discussion or at a formal meeting. It is evidently assumed that formal education will provide helpful background for these "public-speaking" requirements.

Another development, which to me also seems to be a departure from past practices, is the selection of specific trainees for supervisory positions. During the last two or three months over 231 different companies came to the Harvard Business School looking for trainees. Some of the training programs offered by the companies to our graduates were to last as long as three years. These companies sought trainees for supervisory and managerial positions, perhaps not entirely in terms of first-line point of contact with the rank-and-file workers, but probably in the normal course of events that is where a good many of the trainees would have to start.

The point here, however, is that businesses do go outside and select potential supervisors and put them in favorite trainee positions. This practice is somewhat similar to that used by some military services during the war when "90-day wonders" became officers overnight. Often these trainees are supposed to take over the supervision of some rank-and-file people who themselves have been preparing for, and are yearning for, promotion to supervisory positions. Because of the insertion of the trainee group, some of these rank-and-file people may find a promotion blocked or delayed. Thus, it seems to me, that we need to take a look at this trainee practice in terms of what it may do to foster union power and what it may do or may not do to develop teamwork.

Next, what about the training programs for people now in supervisory positions? Generally these programs address themselves to the problem of equipping supervisors with the knowledges and skills, the prestige and authority they are assumed to need to perform their duties and responsibilities.

This problem is approached with varying degrees of effectiveness by training programs. One large company with some 65 different plants has a training program that consists of supervisory training films. In a typical session the supervisors sit and look at a film which pictures an individual who has been working hard and now has arrived at the hallowed goal of having been selected for a supervisory job. Then follows a scene with an individual climbing up a steep hill; coming to the top of that hill, he stands surveying the countryside down below him. This supposedly represents the supervisor's glorious position. He surveys the people who are working for him, and he directs their activities.

I wonder whether we ought not to ask ourselves: How useful is this kind of training in terms of equipping the supervisor with the sort of attitudes which will enable him to cope effectively with union power at the level of the union stewards?

Another significant aspect of these training programs is the emphasis, or reiteration, about being "management-minded." It seems to me that in many cases the aim is to pull down an iron curtain so that the individual trainee will only be able to think on this so-called "management wave length of thinking." Again I should like to ask a question: How useful is such a concept in helping a foreman to deal or cope effectively with a union steward?

Now, let us move to the area of organizational status. What are some of the problems there? In the military forces they often use a characteristic phrase: "Rank has its privileges." The nature of that particular mode of thinking has been or is being transferred to many business organizations where the idea translates itself into job-evaluation programs.

Such job-evaluation programs sometimes include a sort of safety or check factor operating as follows: After the supervisory job has been evaluated, it is reviewed again in terms of how its evaluation results compare money-wise with, say, the average of the highest five people who report to the supervisor. Then if the real job evaluation that results in establishing a standard salary rate does not give a sufficient rating to place it at 25 per cent above the average just mentioned, a higher rating is arbitrarily placed on it to attain this minimum-level salary for a supervisor.

That, it seems to me, almost infuses a double standard in this sense: Originally the idea of job evaluation was that the individual would be paid in terms of, or at any rate his pay was to reflect to some extent, the amount which he contributed to the purposes of the business. This original concept of job evaluation is now superseded by an arbitrary simile of relationships.

Finally, let us take a look at the concept of promotion from within. This is, perhaps, the American dream. It is the sort of thing we like to brag about, and it is the sort of thing that invariably makes an impression on visitors from abroad. I have read several hundred of the Mutual Security Agency and Economic Coöperation Administration reports, and practically every one of them mentions the fact that its writers have met people in managerial positions — plant managers and so on — who had "worked their way up." European visitors consider this a very, very fine achievement and one that differentiates American from European industry and European business organizations.

But it is important to recognize that promotion from within is steadily getting far more difficult. Recently I have talked with a number of the people who came to recruit trainees. I urged them to think in terms of promotion from within, but I recognize that there are certain difficulties. Many industries are now getting to the point where the increased technological knowledge that is required in many cases makes it almost impossible to take an hourly worker and train him for higher positions within the industry.

In summary, then, we come down to the question: How do these personnel practices of selection of trainees, of training programs, of pay and job evaluation, and of promotion from within tend to influence these relationships between union power, teamwork, and management? I believe that we can make the following generalization: The practices that many managements pursue in these four areas may help to foster the sort of climate in which union power will continue to grow, and in such a situation perhaps make it more difficult for teamwork to result from the contact that immediate supervision has with the hourly workers.

Public Policy

We can start on common ground by agreeing that collective bargaining is the accepted policy of our country. It is not only the law of the land, but it is written into the political platforms of both of our major political parties and acclaimed alike by leaders of labor and management.

But we have different ideas of what collective bargaining is. Some people look upon collective bargaining essentially as a poker game, in which both sides play their cards close to their vests. Some regard it as a debating society. Still others look upon it as a slot machine out of which they hope to get more than they put in. Many consider collective bargaining as essentially a power operation, with the rewards going to those who exert the greatest pressure. Finally, others look upon it as a process of reasoning whereby men, reasonable in nature, are persuaded to change their initial positions by facts and evidence. Whatever idea we have of collective bargaining in actual practice, it probably is a composite of all these views.

There would be general agreement, too, that the right to strike or lockout is an integral part of the collective-bargaining process. However, I do not think it is as well recognized that the strike or lockout is a method for *reaching agreement,* and as such fulfills an important function in our society.

When there is a strike or lockout, the minds of both sides may be changed. The workers take a different view of a problem after they have been "on the bricks," and management takes a different view after the plant has been shut down. Fundamental questions which have escaped solution are seen in a clearer perspective, and both sides are impelled to compromise the issues involved.

Now, a real problem lies in those areas of our economy where the right to strike cannot be allowed to be effective because public interest cannot permit the strike to fulfill its function of stimulating agreement. In a mobilization or emergency period, there clearly is an increase in the number of industries and plants where this otherwise proper method of settling disputes cannot be used—for instance, the aircraft industry, or atomic energy plants, or even a particular shipyard. Our problem is to find a substitute for the strike method of producing agreements in these situations. Here it is important to distinguish between two separate questions: (1) How shall we keep essential production going? (2) How shall we settle disputes?

The answer which many businessmen are giving to the question of how to keep essential production going after all voluntary steps have been exhausted is to use the injunction procedure. The Taft-Hartley Act can be called upon, but the injunction is only effective for 80 days; and, as John L. Lewis has shown, it may even be circumvented at the outset by the "individual workers" refusing to abide by the order of the court.

In our society, I suspect that resort to seizure is likely to become the way by which ultimately essential production is continued. The point is that seizure works. On one side, the property is in government hands and management cannot protest. On the other side, it is part of our general mores as a country that you do not strike against the government. I do not mean that we should not try to maintain essential production by a combination of means, including voluntary extension of contracts and even injunction in some cases, but I want to point out that ultimately we may have to resort to seizure. If the President does not have the power to seize in cases like that of the steel companies, then clearly the Congress of the United States should afford the President that right, with appropriate safeguards for the companies and unions.

But all this is no answer to the question of how to *settle* the dispute — a wholly different question. Here we must keep in mind the old adage, "You can lead a horse to water, but you can't make him drink." The only conclusive way to settle disputes is by agreement. We may use a lot of intermediate devices, such as mediation, arbitration, fact-finding boards, and recommendations, but the agreement process must be the final step.

The steel crisis has shown us more clearly than ever before that we must sharpen our focus on this problem of essential industry in a mobilization period. For the problem is not just one of finding the machinery to assure continuation of production; we must also take into account the fact that agreement is the end result to be achieved. Injunctions or seizures only serve to permit the continuation of operations while settlement is being brought about. For example, we have recently completed the settlement of a series of disputes in the railroad industry, which started in the fall of 1950; a seizure took place at that time, but the facilities were not returned to the railroads until agreement was reached in 1952.

Another major current problem in the area of public policy is that of the relationship between collective bargaining and stabilization. There is no doubt that stabilization interferes to a certain degree with collective bargaining. An agreement which the parties enter into may be upset by the stabilization agency, and there will certainly be disputes which arise during a period of stabilization and which involve the application of stabilization policies.

In this connection it is important to distinguish certain types of disputes. Some disputes are over what the regulations or policies mean in a particular case. What is the amount that may be allowable under the regulations in relation to particular sets of facts? Other disputes stem from uncertainty whether the particular stabilization policies are applicable in the case or whether an exception should be made to the general rules. Then, there are disputes which directly challenge the regulations themselves.

In a stabilization program it is desirable to have the coöperation of labor and industry. Indeed, it is impossible to operate such a program without the effective participation and coöperation of both sides. For what we have had during the emergency is actually a limited form of a no-strike commitment. The labor leaders of the country have, in effect, said: "We will not exercise the right to strike which we have and which has not been curtailed in any way. We will not exercise that right to strike for wage increases *outside the limits of the stabilization program.*"

In the absence of that kind of commitment, a stabilization program would quickly run into the problem of what to do when a strike is directed against the stabilization program. An all-public board, for example, would very quickly fail upon that particular issue, in my conviction, because the strike would really be a strike against public policy.

To summarize what I have said up to this point, I would take the view that the strike is an integral part of collective bargaining; that in these times we need to distinguish between methods to assure the continuation of production and methods to settle the dispute; and that if we are to take away or limit the right to strike, then we must have substitutes for this method of settling disputes.

I have also tried to suggest that a stabilization program and collective bargaining are, to a certain degree, in conflict, which means that the coöperation and active participation of labor and management people are needed to solve the central problem of continuing production and avoiding strikes and stoppages.

Perhaps the most crucial single issue raised by the whole steel situation is whether the machinery that we are to use in this country for the handling of emergency disputes will be developed by the leaders of labor and management together, along the lines of the collective bargaining process, or whether it will be imposed by politicians.

My own personal view is that the joint development of such

machinery is vastly to be desired, and the absence of it will strike a fundamental blow at the future development of collective bargaining. We need to get the leaders of management and labor together on the question of what machinery they can agree upon for the handling of these emergency disputes.

Conflict and Resolution

American business is missing a historical opportunity. Seldom—indeed I may say never—has an industrial group been confronted with an organized labor group at once so powerful and so nonrevolutionary as that in the United States today. American labor embodies the most conservative type of union organization in the world. Ours is the only nation with a powerful labor movement which does not base its thinking, in some respects, on Karl Marx.

Let Great Britain furnish the characteristic example, with its traditions of civic freedoms rooted in the Magna Charta, which of course enter into our own Anglo-American heritage. For British labor pursues a moderate kind of socialistic program, not the revolutionary type of socialism. Yet its works remain the product of a socialism based on the nationalization of basic industries. The government, unlike Russia, pays a "fair price," determined by arbitration, when it takes those industries over. But, when all the qualifications are marshaled, present-day British labor constitutes a recognized socialistic movement.

In our country, our ancestors came from many countries and all sorts of people. This proved a fortunate and dynamic factor in our development. The hardy and ambitious immigrants, absorbed into a free society on a richly endowed continent, assumed also for their children the first great society free of rigid class structure. Briefly after the Civil War, it is true, as industrialization swept through our country and industries began to struggle for social control, Karl Marx's ideas gained some popularity. After 1872, indeed, Karl Marx moved his headquarters to New York, and splinter "sections" of the First International appeared in other large American cities. And

Karl Marx himself, let us note, even became a correspondent of the New York *Tribune*!

But Marxian socialism never sank real roots. Not only the character of American economy, but also that of the men who rose to labor leadership militated against its growth. Union builders like Samuel Gompers (as his *Autobiography* explicitly testifies) consciously revalued — and rejected — the Marxian program for American democracy.

> This need not — and will not — be our way [they decided]. This too we left behind when we crossed the Atlantic Ocean. We will organize unions and deal with employers on wages, hours, and conditions. But for us too the American standard of living, of increasing plenty for free men, remains the moving goal. Toward this end, we affirm our recognition of rights to private property and, indeed, seek always to hold to a minimum government intervention in industrial relations.

Our labor leaders have been Jeffersonians who fitted that founding father's fear of omnipresent government to the new concerns of an urban industrial society.

Basically, the philosophy of American labor even to this day has undergone little fundamental change. As the CIO really got going in the 1930's, it looked for a while as if labor's strategies might take on a more radical tinge; and in the tumult of 1937 we did see plant barricades, sit-down strikes, and all that such developments might imply.

But, looking back now upon these turbulent times, we begin to realize also that during the Roosevelt Administration and the war period we navigated the "ship of state" full steam ahead safely through stormy waters. World events at the same time were revealing that the "Marxian way" can add up to reaction. We were saved from our own potential variant of this throwback to absolutism in big government. It is true we also made many changes, but by now it is clear that not only union labor but also practically all Americans thereby peacefully changed course in assimilating social security, farm parity, savings insurance, and so on, into the American way of life. From the brief Marxist revolutionary potential of the sit-downs, we turned, even reversed the drift, to find ourselves passing into full employment and amicable adjustment formulae like the War Labor Board's maintenance of membership — not the union shop but maintenance of membership — to find ourselves, in a word, American people as always making their opportunities to work and earn a "good" living.

From some fifteen million unemployed we have come through the test of world war to unsurpassed strength. From situations which always make for potential revolution, because men will not let their wives and kids starve if agitators offer alternatives, we have emerged to the orderly procedures of evolving collective bargaining, with the newer leadership of the CIO gradually turning toward the same philosophy that the older AFL leadership had carried forward by gradual adjustments to changing circumstance.

This expansion within historic courses was epitomized by the Lewis-Taylor agreement. That agreement averted a dangerous struggle. Little Steel was engulfed in upheavals, and tragedy threatened in 1937 when that strike evoked bloodshed in Chicago. But John L. Lewis and Myron C. Taylor disintegrated the looming thrust of profound conflict by marking out new alternatives. Instead of trying to go back to 1919 and its intransigent ideas of individualism, in 1937 Big Steel no longer affirmed management's right to maintain even benevolent (but exclusive) power. Its policymakers no longer insisted: "We alone protect our workers; our own workers alone deal with us. Our workers need no outside power to intervene for them with us."

Instead, Big Steel signed the agreement, and, to my mind, America averted potential tragedy. Certainly this great industry, as well as other unionized sectors, did not eliminate all differences and difficulties in building collective relations with its now organized workers. As recently as mid-1951 the steel industry was again shut down, even though the issues still dividing the "parties" seemed so minor — issues as to the form of recognition, the monies to be paid for work, the pennies per hour, and so on. But from any long-term point of view the character of these issues "between the parties" held their own reassurance. In America, these powerful protagonists of management and labor differed over the familiar issues of "wages, hours, and conditions"—and in resolving those differences they were hewing out orderly procedures by which even the strike could be faced as a concrete mutual and communal problem. We seek ways together to handle and curb such emergency shutdowns; no considerable sector of our workers echo European or Eastern revolutionaries in wielding strikes and unrest as instruments of revolutionary upheaval.

CIO development over the postwar years confirms this judgment. Steadily through the stresses of testing their new power in the uncertain economy of these past seven years or so, the leaders of the new mass unions, wielding often real industry-wide power, have cast their programs increasingly within the familiar—yet still dynamic—American molds. Certainly, as far as fundamental challenges to private ownership of property and management rights provide the crucial measure, the new and evolving CIO is just as conservative as the old and also evolving AFL. Because both *are* evolving, management retains its opportunity to influence the industrial directions along which we shall move in the years ahead.

Consider from this whole viewpoint the General Motors contract. Who would have thought Walter Reuther would sign, in 1950, even before Korea, a five-year contract according to which he would have nothing to say about production and would agree to define criteria for orderly wage movements. The agreement takes on renewed significance against the realities of the union's power in that full-employment market. For Reuther agreed to forego the recurrent drama of battling for maximum wage increases by setting limits on job rates he might wring by bargaining techniques from a favorable market.

The real significance of this agreement lay in the recognition which each party signatory to it finally gave to the "legitimacy" of the power claimed by the other. It is essential that we all recognize and rethink these issues of legitimate power. Certainly no human affairs can be organized without having defined loci of power. Someone has to make decisions. But if those decisions can be challenged within defined limits and by defined procedure, neither the initiator nor the challenger need lose effective authority. Together they modify the going power structure; unlike the "revolutionists" of our day, they do not build a more absolute, unchallengeable one.

We always think of *labor*—that is, European labor—as being the revolutionists of our time. I think *businessmen*—and particularly American businessmen—are our biggest revolutionists. They are the innovators who set in motion the basic changes that transform life: new industries, new products, and new plants (moving from here to there, following the natural resources, changing the location of mills, drawing upon new sources of labor). Plants must be opened, expanded, shut down as demand changes, as political and judicial decisions alter the circumstances to which business functioning must adjust. From the other side, if industrialists bring in, say, 175,000 laborers to meet a "labor shortage," perhaps 10 per cent or 15 per cent of them being Puerto Ricans or other ethnic minorities, and if these same industrialists subsequently feel it necessary for good business reasons to close their plants and pull out, how do they expect those workers to get along? Consequences pile up; the police stations get to know a lot of the stranded workers very well; juvenile delinquents emerge from the family dislocations; new pressure groups appear in the political lobbies; and so on.

We talk about the industrial revolution. It really was a businessman's, a commercial man's, revolution. In the beginning there was the application of science to the production of goods; the laboratory and the scientists were put into the factory, so to speak. But the expansion of markets for expanded products had to be closely tied up with this change. In the United States, it may well have come first; and, ultimately, industrial democratic society has emerged as a new historic phenomenon, a society of potential mass abundance for free men.

Why, then, do you think Karl Marx found so many ready ears in Europe? Certainly not because *Das Kapital* is easy to read. Instead, his message has had continuously to be translated, reduced to shibboleths. Its conceptual underpinning is a structure of subtle complexities, cumbersome forms, big words. Few of those ardent European Communists who compose the fighting ranks have ever read Karl Marx.

But Marx generalized the first impact of industrialism. He paid his meed of tribute to the technological accomplishments of business, applying the secrets of science to production, making goods for service, transportation, housing. He saw the potential for higher living standards created by business. But he also speculated upon an unchanging power hierarchy *in* industrial society. He did not see beyond the exploitation, the truly terrific, exploitation of the mid-nineteenth century. Watching women and children haul coal carts, he decried the reformers seeking labor laws and the prosaic workingmen writing prosaic collective agreements.

But businessmen themselves today "see" what Marx missed. They see counterpower. They see human beings with brains and feelings. You can push them around only so much; then they band together for protection. First, they form local societies and local groups and, finally, national unions. Where women and children once hauled coal carts, men like John L. Lewis now hurl thunderbolts.

Power was inherent early in industrial situations, just as a different structure of power is imminent in today's industrial relations. But looking back we can see that we could not have had our economic progress with the symbolic economic royalists like Gary, Frick, and Carnegie. Perhaps that past age of managerial power underlies our present potential for abundance. Who can say, for example, whether it was not a good thing that the CIO did not get going before 1930? For if recognized unionization had spread from the AFL, say, in the period of the first World War, we might not have been able to organize mass production on the American model in industry and hence might never have had its benefits.

In earlier industry, each craftsman at the machines worked with 25 or 30 other craftsmen. Jurisdictional fighting and jousting as to who should have this or who should have that was not confined to the building trades. Yes, it is a fortunate thing we got mass production going before mass unionism. At any rate, by the time mass unionism emerged with the CIO, the patterns of work and technological advance under the initiating power of managerial leaders like Du Pont, Ford, Grace, Wilson, and the others who controlled basic industries were crystallized. Conclusive demonstration came with the challenge of war. American industry turned out to be the savior not only of our democracy but also of the whole free world.

The arsenal of democracy once more proved to be American mass production. And, since 1945, as former enemies became present-day allies and former allies present-day enemies, the continuing struggle in the arena of international power — the cold war, if you will — is proving to be a struggle in industrial preparedness.

Perhaps that is why we Americans still have no sense of our own real power. Our long-time experience has been one of growth and industrial maturing. In that growing process, however, our basic endowments of human stock, natural resources, and technologic skill spelled also inherent strength, strength so massive that even in 1953 we can assimilate the mistakes we make and still go on. When crisis recurrently arises, the potential for rising to crisis remains. No nation yet can compare with us as far as inherent power is concerned.

And, so, I return to my original proposition that American business is missing a wonderful opportunity. Do we face the world's most powerful labor movement? We face also the one pursuing the most conservative objectives in our time of upheaval — objectives completely within the American tradition. Our labor unions demand rising standards of living, better conditions, more fringe benefits, opportunity to be heard — that is, opportunity to bar both foremen and company presidents from pushing union workers around — freedom to strike if they think a strike is necessary to their interest, opportunity to go fishing, too, and opportunity to educate their children and to send them to Harvard College if they want to! (I am always heartened to see how many boys in the Harvard Business School come from workingmen's families.)

What, then, does all this, in concrete terms, demand of business leaders during these uncertain days of social transition? For one thing, we must recognize the legitimacy of power. We have to recognize first that we ourselves have power and are not to be ashamed of it. We have to accept the fact that the other guy with whom we have to deal has the same right to be organized on a power basis too.

Gone forever are the relatively clear-cut days we look back upon — the days when laborers constituted a variable cost, a flexible supply that moved up and down in each given plant with business conditions, when no voluntary or contractual commitments toward the union interfered on this sector of cost accounting. Yet managers still retain power to move plants from the North to the South and to import labor from Puerto Rico, men who must go back to Puerto Rico or go on insurance and relief when the business boom is over. Can we not fairly say that such consequences — and many others — belong to the price the whole nation has paid for the dynamism of its great economy? But within this same framework the allocation of these social costs can also be accepted as proper issues for negotiation among all economic groups. Those who have power in one era must be prepared to accommodate to redistribution of group power in another.

This simply means that, if businessmen require — inherently — the power to make those daily decisions which over the years have operated the continuous revolution by which poverty is being abolished and living standards raised, then they rightly fight to preserve that power. But other economic groups must, by the same token, be granted legitimate power to scrutinize the full impact of those decisions.

Indeed, a strange thing begins to happen in the new power setup. It becomes evident that responsibility for unpleasant consequences can be shared.

Such sharing of responsibility is based on recognition that the harsh decisions business must now and again make are often inescapable. Advancing technology displaces skilled men; declining demand necessitates layoffs; regional shifts induce plant relocations; and so on. Unless what must be done technically and economically is done, everyone loses in the long run. Excess sense of guilt in these matters, as in any relationships, cripples ultimate effectiveness; toughmindedness need not be hardheartedness.

Yet no one who has known individual businessmen well can believe they always face these difficult decisions, with their human consequences, lightly. I have known, as we all have known, individual businessmen who quailed, even during the stressful days of the Great Depression, before the ineluctable layoffs had to be authorized. In the generally prosperous 1920's when some consumption goods industries similarly confronted necessary technologic displacements, one such business leader, well known to us at the Business School, sought for a humane way to effect these harsh inevitabilities. Significantly he found it in coöperating with the union with which his company had been dealing for many years. The union recognized that part of this company's ability to survive, stay in business, and thus provide jobs for members was determined by how it met its cost factors, in terms of advancing technology among other things.

By and large, most American unions accept technology. They argue the incidence of change; but they accept its long-run national beneficence. The short-run factors only are subject to negotiation. Thus it has been that, after bitter, violent strikes for recognition, once a company has said, "We *are* going to recognize this group of leaders as having legitimate powers which we first challenged," working relationships have improved and orderly procedures for adjusting and resolving differences have emerged.

Naturally, most of us do not like to have power taken away from us. It is easier to exercise exclusive power, to affirm intention to wield that power "for the benefit of all," without thinking too much about what that means. We can say that authority comes from the bottom, but down in our hearts we know that, when the chips are down, we on the top have the authority. We may have to listen to others if necessary, but we do have the last word. There is a difference between that sort of thing and facing somebody who really can make you listen enough to modify the first course that might have been chosen.

To my mind — and I try to identify the thought with the man who must act — if I am going to have great responsibility in running an industry, I *want* somebody "on the other side" who can make me listen and face all the implications even of necessary action. I think I can do business with that fellow who has shown every day that he can make me listen.

Toward this end American managements must continuously ask themselves whether deep down in their hearts they have ever really accepted unions. One of the disservices that the human relations approach may yet do is to leave some people with the feeling that unions do not have to exist. I would say you cannot in this day have a General Motors without a union, or a Ford without a union, or a United States Steel without a union. It isn't in the present-day cards. Some economists have been arguing that modern unionism cannot coexist, cannot prove "compatible," with modern capitalism. I would say, rather, that we today cannot have capitalism without having unions.

So the first thing we have to do is to accept unions and let them know and feel that they are accepted. Such acceptance will end a great deal of trouble between union officials and executives.

Since the depression, formal acceptance has spread. But, for our first experience with large-scale collective bargaining, since 1941, we have found ourselves living in an inflationary period with full employment. Neither in the second World War, nor in the Korean War have we been honestly willing to have a stabilization program which would fix prices as of a certain day and leave them frozen. The businessmen do not want that. The farmers do not want that. The unions have said they would take stabilization *if* everybody else did; but I am not so sure.

Reduced to the concrete realities of daily living, the economy never functions in a vacuum: we go into a war, or an emergency, and men become aware of what they call conclusively — for their own aims — "inequities." People continue to be motivated in traditional ways. The man who has developed a nonferrous industry still feels pressure to make some money out of it. If he wants to attract workers, he does it by offering them more money than another mill or locality or industry — if he can. Financial incentives remain essentially the driving motivation; and, frankly, that is the reason we have never, any of us, wanted to have a "freeze."

It may seem as if the British, shall we say, to cite one example, have shown themselves more willing to accept the exigent pervasive requirements of true stabilization. But the patriotic Britons simply stabilized against different circumstances from those confronting equally patriotic Americans. Britons, facing invasion first and bankruptcy later, rationed the sacrifices imposed by true scarcity. They furthered a peaceful social transition at the same time. Americans knew war and economic stresses too; but they faced them from the relative warmth of strength, security, and growing abundance.

Be that as it may, war or great national stress brings inevitably some measure of inflation — here hidden, there explicitly measured; here controlled, there tragically uncontrolled. In the United States too, since 1940, we have been pouring capital and resources into armaments and other goods. The workers who make them have money to buy more than the markets make available to consumers generally. When there are not enough goods for consumers who have the money to buy, inflation is inevitable. Thus the realities that have bedeviled us in trying to work new power relationships as well as human relationships have stemmed from this inevitable inflation. Perplexed by the hard enough complexities of accommodating to new social facts, we have found outlets for the natural rancors evoked by burgeoning labor in the concomitant rigors of inflationary economics.

But once we see inflation as a consequence of every war in our history, we are less sure that if only the new union wage pressure were relaxed or obviated, our inflation would end.

Indeed, no labor leader could last one day if he relaxed the pressure to keep wages abreast of prices, as his members "see" inflation. Only when adverse conditions, such as are prevalent right now in the textile and clothing industries, exist in the understandable terms of "bad business" can union spokesmen accommodate policy to stable wages or less in times like these. Elsewhere there is full-time activity and people are being hired; by what argument can workers be persuaded to lead the procession to forbearance? Stabilization must be a communal program, framed for the community as a whole and carried by all alike.

Within the "voluntary framework" of collective bargaining, big industry today explores two roads, what we may term, broadly, the "G. M." way and the "steel" way.

General Motors predicated its case for orderly wage adjustment by agreed criteria, in terms of logic that explicitly embodied the major case Reuther and other union people had long been urging for wage increases: living costs and living standards. But it presented that case in the format of a bargaining table proposal that was at once logical and long term — a nondisruptive way of handling the wage issue as it developed over a protracted contract term. It said to employees:

> First, you are entitled in time of full employment to have your wages keep up with the rise in consumer prices and the cost of living; secondly, since we want you to be interested in productivity, we will see that you get, every year, about 2% of your wages as an increase.

The company and the union signed the contract; and, in time, Ford, Chrysler, and other automotive concerns signed similar contracts. Projected before Korea, this wage regulation which has come to be known as the G. M. formula represents a real social invention by voluntary legislation in industrial self-government. It may prove still to be inadequate in detail or for the short term; yet it remains democratic experimentation in a new realm.

In steel, reliance remains with the older patterns of tug and tussle by traditional collective bargaining. At the close of each contract term, or the dawn of each "wage reopening period," cost-of-living figures are differentially scanned by the two parties. Says the corporation: "No, let us keep wages and prices as they are. If steelworkers forbear, the companies will not ask price increases and we will curb inflation." Says the union: "Prices *have* gone up; we trail the procession; steel should lead, not lag." Actually in the total context of inflationary forces, wages do go up; but their rise is only a secondary factor which follows after the real inflationary forces have been set in motion.

Somehow both sides at each negotiation table must adjust to that reality even as they also participate in a national effort to stabilize. Otherwise, as in steel, there erupts periodic trouble: in 1946, in 1948, in 1950, and 1952!

The shouting and tumult of these familiar wage conflicts, however, should not blur for us the overriding reality of present-day American experience. We have already achieved a classless society, including a union movement, without bloody warfare. The one issue we are facing now is how to develop further and continue to widen the distribution of our wealth, in which there is the great potential of mass abundance. The traditional wage conflict would become a minor one if our businessmen would really develop this historical insight, would really understand the labor movement for what it is in this country — a conservative, nonrevolutionary movement — and thus would not alienate labor spokesmen like the late Philip Murray.

But what about that second issue of principle and power as the companies have defined it: the union shop. I go around and see companies with 85 per cent or 90 per cent of the people belonging to the union; I see some where the figure is even as low as 65 per cent or 70 per cent. Ever more widely, however, union dues are sent off by the companies to the union treasury. Modifying formulae may be broached; yet even in steel there is a union shop in existence in all but name. This is true of United States Steel, Bethlehem, Republic, and on down the roll. Does it not seem that on this issue, too, a modifying formula from the start might have served the industry in 1952 better than an affirmative of absolutist "principle"?

For, from the union point of view, some variant of the union shop apparently still seems to be *a must.* In labor's vivid recollection this remains the one country where unions failed to gain more than a foothold until the 1930's. Out of that struggle they survived; but also out of that struggle the union shop, the closed shop — some device for security and control — took form as an instrument of sheer survival.

Thus it is that in our time the union shop issue remains a mark of union legitimacy; and management may as well accept the situation in terms of such social symbolism. Most big industries indeed, to repeat, do now grant the union shop and the checkoff; and that is one way of giving assurance of enduring acceptance to the unions.

Within the shelter of such "top acceptance," sound relationships develop between local supervisors and the union fellows. Consider steel itself as an example. I was in a town where one of the major steel companies maintains some of its biggest mills. It was 1952, and the workers were asking: "Will the Supreme Court render the decision against seizure and what should we do? Will there be a strike?

Shall we be involved?" They were involved as we now know. But, once again, this did not spell fierce drawing of lines between the management inside and the strikers outside. Instead, local management made available to the men — as the men themselves told me — "a tent at the gate for pickets to use if it rains or the sun gets hot"; electric wires were strung from the power station to provide electric light; "coffee and doughnuts" — refreshments — were served.

The significant point emerges that this has become the repeating pattern for handling strikes in this steel town. Local supervision and local union men told me their new story proudly. They nodded when I commented, "Quite a change from 1937!" This, too, even at strike time, they realized, represents conservative teamwork, coöperation, and goodwill, which carries through continuing mill relationships.

Let us then conclude as we began. We possess a wonderful historical opportunity to get away from these hostilities of minor issues, to be aware of the power we have in the way statesmen are aware of power. Statesmen deal with power all the time. And it is statesmanship to know how to handle power, to know when to negotiate and when not to negotiate, to know when to accommodate or when to "take" a strike.

John R. Commons, a professor of some years ago and one of the greatest economists who ever lived in this country, said that in every transaction there are three elements in our kind of democracy: (1) *difference of opinion* — even *conflict,* perhaps without which you cannot have competition in a free enterprise society; (2) *mutuality;* and (3) *resolution,* resulting from the play between mutuality and conflict.[1] In our kind of society there is no one final, beautiful resolution. There is only continuous transacting, because our society is dynamic. We must have continuous differences between groups; but we do also have continuous mutuality. By that token, if we define the actual concrete issues successively before us with practical realism, we will also work out successful resolutions in the traditional manner of American nonrevolutionary advance.

[1] See Benjamin M. and Sylvia K. Selekman, "An Economics for Administrators," *Harvard Business Review,* XXIX, No. 6 (November 1951), p. 112.

DEVELOPING AND MAINTAINING THE EXECUTIVE TEAM

Edmund P. Learned, Ross G. Walker, Andrew R. Towl, and George A. Smith, Jr.

Administration

One who has had the experience of being part of an organization knows what a tremendous job it is to find the right kind of people, attract them to the organization, keep them after getting them, train them, build up their strengths, play down their shortcomings, and get them to work together. In any organization most people work in what might be called a small administrative unit, whether it is a factory unit, a sales unit, an office unit, or a spot toward the top of the chain of organization.

Every person in one of these administrative units has a personality and an integrity that he seeks to protect, and he brings to the work place, whether it is at the executive level or at the bottom level, all his background of experience at home, at school, or at play. That background of experience conditions his capacity to learn and thereby creates one of the minor problems of communication which you have in any business, whether it be large or small.

Each of these persons seeks to obtain individuality or protection of personality and recognition within his own administrative group. He has his own personal aspirations, goals, or objectives, and they may or may not be identical with those of the rest of the group. As administrators we have to think of the objectives of the organization, but we cannot forget that the individuals who are parts of our ad-

NOTE: Mr. Learned is Professor of Business Administration, Mr. Walker is Professor of Business Administration, Mr. Towl is Assistant Director of Research, and Mr. Smith is Professor of Business Administration, Harvard Business School.

Mr. Learned explains the problems of administration; Mr. Walker discusses the Advanced Management Program; Mr. Towl deals with executive compensation; and Mr. Smith provides the conclusion.

ministrative units also have personal objectives which have to be taken into account.

It is wholly legitimate and normal for people to ask the basic question, "What does this mean to me?" Every action or potential action inside an organization is measured first, whether consciously or unconsciously, by the individual in terms of this question. In other words, most people like to seek new targets of personal opportunity inside the organization for which they are working, and they want freedom to achieve and express their personality.

What is the administrative significance of this fundamental point? I think it implies that it is possible to release the creative power and the expression of personality and personal growth inside an administrative organization if the administrative leader creates the right atmosphere.

During the last year or two that Elton Mayo was on the Faculty of the Harvard Business School, it was my privilege to associate with him more intimately than when I first joined the staff. From him I learned something of the psychological doctrines he had developed, particularly what has come to be known as "the doctrine of complications" and the "doctrine of personal growth." I think he would have agreed that if we release this desire of people to grow as individuals within the organization environment, and if we help them to understand our objectives and, in turn, we try to understand theirs, then we have gone a long way in solving the problems of morale and satisfaction.

To achieve this goal, the administrative leader — at both the executive level and the supervisory level — must have face-to-face contact with people in order to understand the individual differences and the individual ways of expressing personality and character. In other words, an organizational unit should never be so large that the person in charge does not have the opportunity of knowing individuals *as* individuals, because to a great extent this opportunity affects his capacity to deal with the problem of the group and the problems of the business.

I think an organization becomes an organization when the administrative leaders are tied together in terms of common objectives. In a sense I am suggesting that individuals think first of themselves. They may or may not tend to develop a group loyalty. And somehow or other, if you are going to get the job of the world done in an organized way, these individuals and these small groups have to be tied together. It is particularly important, therefore, that administrative leaders be able to understand the members of the individual group and to understand what makes an organization.

It is only after these groups are tied together that we begin to make progress. Upon the administrative leader of the small group rests the responsibility for a basically sound organization. It is he who is actually going to interpret up and down the organization the objectives of the company and the aspirations and capabilities of the people in it. He has to do this in personal terms in order to develop individual understanding. He has a horizon expanding beyond that of his particular activities; it is his business to interrelate his activities and those of his group with other activities throughout the organization.

Moving up to the executive level to make another point, I think that men at the top set an example not by their words but by their behavior. An important characteristic of human nature is the desire to please the boss. Therefore, there is an automatic tendency for us to give the superior what he wants as long as he holds so much of our future in his hands.

If the executive has high standards of work, he will get high standards of work. If he has sloppy standards of performance, he will get sloppy work. This has nothing to do with the question of discipline or poor human relations. You can have wonderful human relations and still not have high standards.

If the executive believes in teamwork, he can get teamwork by example. I well remember one of the key cases in our Business Policy course, in which there was a president working with vice-presidents on a man-to-man basis, which of course is a desirable thing. But he would talk about a general policy problem with only one executive at a time, not with the whole group of executives who had an interest in the matter, and make his decision. He would then talk to another vice-president about another matter and make another decision. And so on. He kept in his own hands all the coördinating activity.

I recall another case where a president asked a vice-president for a recommendation, but failed to ask him whether he had consulted with other executives about their concern with this particular matter. The vice-president had in fact not attempted such coördination and understanding, and so the resulting decision of the president was a poor one. If that president had done as other presidents have done in other cases and said to the first vice-president, "Have you talked to this man and that man and that man?" and if he had waited for an affirmative answer before he took action, at least the vice-president would have sought the advice of his assistants the next time that a problem of broad implications came up.

Let us consider the question of executive teamwork in the problem of line-and-staff relationships. I have found that staff men in a great many businesses tend to be frustrated because they have no formal authority. They have no power except the power of persuasion. But sometimes staff men work for an executive who uses them as if they were line officers — there are plenty of companies where that practice is generally accepted — and it is in such situations that frustration really ensues, especially among the line executives who resent staff men acting as bosses.

In business it is essential to fix responsibility, authority, and accountability. We talk about organization charts and we talk about procedures, and all those things make a contribution to effective teamwork. But not many problems at the executive level are exclusively within the jurisdiction of a single functional vice-president or other executive officer. Problems have a way of cutting across lines of organizational responsibility.

If this is true, the question arises: "How can we fix the responsibility for a solution?" That is where I come back to the formal organization chart and the doctrine of primary responsibility as a key to one good solution.

I like to think of executives or department heads as a team, each with some primary responsibility. A certain individual is told, "You are responsible for the marketing function." But marketing has relationships with production, with transportation, and with many other things, as we all know. Or, "You are in charge of production." But production has ramifications extending far beyond its immediate applications.

Now assume a business problem of broad significance. It should be assigned to some office for solution. I would suggest that we make the problem the focal point of our attack, that we assign it to the officer or office of primary responsibility or major interest, that we conceive of the people who can make a contribution to a wise business solution of that problem as a sort of an informal task force to be drawn around the problem, and that we think of the officer or office of primary responsibility as the leader of this task force.

Much of the organization rivalry and lack of teamwork would disappear if the leaders at the executive level could help their organizations focus on problem-solutions and the development of procedures for interrelationships and could bring to problems those men best able to solve them regardless of what department they belong to. Such men in the so-called task force will get a kick out of solving problems coöperatively rather than building up an exclusive status for their organization unit.

Certain executives whom I consider great artists in business administration, and some in government too, are using this approach. This is like committee management in a way. But I am very dubious about committees that spend all their time debating.

I am advocating general management solutions rather than narrow departmental ones. In a sense this task force concept resembles a committee setup, but in an informal way. You can get just as good results working informally as you can formally; it is the attitude of mind that is important. As a matter of fact, I think good committees, if you use that form of management, require good chairmen; and if you have a good chairman, it adds up to my proposal because a good chairman has got to farm out jobs. Otherwise the debating continues ad infinitum with no result.

I think the great values to any organization from spelling out organizational manuals, job descriptions, and interrelationships are found more in the process of doing than in the end result. These are ways of developing understanding of the interconnections and interrelationships within an organization. In my opinion — and I do not intend to reflect on the experienced consulting firms — the values are mostly realized while the process is going on; this I want to emphasize.

In any organization where you have a fairly high turnover of people, you need broad policy statements, and you may need some specific records of actions that you have taken. In organizations with rapid turnover, in fact, you may need much more elaborate manuals of procedure so that people will know what to do, with whom, when, and (to some extent) why. On the other hand, if you prescribe in too much detail, then you have reduced the area of personal growth and personal interpretation.

A well-defined, meticulously drawn organization chart is either desirable or undesirable depending on the character of the executives. If you have a strong executive group, secure in their attitudes and positions, an arbitrary organization chart is probably unnecessary and a hindrance. On the other hand, with an executive or a group of executives who do not feel secure, an organization chart may become indispensable. Here is an example suggested by a businessman:

Ours is an organization of about 400 people, a typical manufacturing concern which has important engineering as well as production problems. There is a production head who has come up through the whole organization — an extremely capable man with a thorough sense of security in his job and in the respect in which he is held. He cares nothing for an organization chart himself, and he is perfectly willing to have other people go around him to his subordinates. He doesn't feel that he needs the protection of a complete, highly organized line of authority.

The chief engineer, on the other hand, is and always has been the sort of individual who cannot work well in an organization; and out of this there has grown a clear, obvious sense of personal insecurity. If we violate the organization chart as far as he is concerned, this man becomes very much upset. It is unwise to go around him. It is unwise to take a free and easy approach with his subordinates, to do things in an informal way in the interests of speed or rapid interchange of ideas.

In other words, he must have the organization chart, whereas the other man doesn't need it at all.

What I am really after is the sort of relationship described by William B. Given in the March–April 1952 issue of the *Harvard Business Review* in an article, "Reaching Out in Management." But it is not an easy thing to achieve, especially in an organization that has been static for a long time, with the same people in the same jobs and executives not used to operating in this way.

Patterns do get established and are hard to break. The executive has to recognize that time and great patience, plus setting a very good personal example, are needed. If the company has always worked in closely restricted lines of responsibility and the decision is suddenly made to develop a little more of the teamwork approach in cutting across lines, then the top executive has got to take stock of himself. Probably he is responsible for the too-rigid pattern because that is the way he has been working.

One of the steps in changing it would be to call in his key vice-presidents to discuss an issue of general policy, admitting that conditions could stand improvement. The first thing they would probably say when they came out of the office would be, "What's come over the boss?" They would think he has had an off day, and they would speculate about what caused it. If he repeated his tactics three or four times, they would think, without any comment on his part, "Something has happened." And in a little while they too would loosen up. If he is a wise man and is trying to bring about the change, he would probably choose a problem which he can farm out to the various responsible organization elements for a solution.

If you delegate down in an organization to people who have some capacity to solve a problem and they come up with successful solutions, their success will aid their personal growth and satisfactions in the organization. In other words, if you keep job responsibilities frozen, you fail to capitalize on growth potential. I call this concept "dynamic responsibility." Executives should get their satisfaction out of creating organizations that can *do,* rather than out of making all the decisions themselves.

A Lesson in Training Techniques

In presenting this lesson in training techniques I may seem to be advertising one of the Harvard Business School's enterprises. But the fact is that our Advanced Management Program (AMP) has turned out to be so different from any previous educational experiment in training executives — and indeed so different from what we ourselves expected — that I know of no other way to illustrate the points I think should be made.

To begin with, I should like to look back to that bit of the program's history just following the war when the wisdom of continuing it was in question. Those were interesting days. A lot of people thought that the program would just naturally fold up and quietly disappear with its records into the School's archives. And of course it was not unreasonable at the time to take for granted that this particular kind of adult education had simply run its course.

The war was over, and the program had finished its job of serving as an aid in training for better skills in production management, that is, as a tool of war, for which, back in 1941, it had been originally designed by the Government and the School. "The war is over, let's forget it," was the attitude. Even the Dean's office, as I remember things, agreed with the Faculty and others in taking a dim view of the future of this special kind of training. Even though as far back as September 1943 a committee of the Faculty had reviewed its merits as a continuing and "integral part" of the School's operations, and had concluded that with a suitable broadening of scope it could easily make a permanent place for itself in the University, such was the sentiment right after the war.

Not only was this surface logic for ending the program convincing, but people, tired from the war, readily succumbed to the plausible argument that, after all, the proper aim of the Harvard Business School was the education of youngsters — that the degree of Master of Business Administration was the true "core" of its contribution to society — and that the sooner the Faculty got back to this main business the better.

But as soon as our feelings about the future of this experiment in adult education began to be understood away from the School, in business, and among competent and influential observers of the School's activities, dozens of protesting letters and calls began to come in. Their message was that apparently we at the School had not as yet awakened to what a big and significant thing this Advanced Management Program had come to be in business; and that, while of course the operation would have to be rebuilt in many respects to fit long-run, peacetime needs, its effects on the students had proved to be much broader than its mere initial design or narrow war purposes would indicate possible, besides suggesting enormous further contributions to follow upon proper redesigning. Many people who were entitled to voice an opinion on matters of executive development even went so far as to indicate their sincere belief that this broad kind of schooling of experienced older men had come in fact to displace the Master of Business Administration Program for men just out of college as the sort of activity through which this School could best serve the interests of American business and society.

Now what did these people, responsible businessmen, fear that they would be losing, or that business and society would be losing, if the School made the decision to abandon the Advanced Management Program with the close of the war?

In general the story from business was that, although as yet management did not know very much about how to build executives — was in fact just beginning to lay out formal plans for the purpose — everybody was sure of one thing, namely, that in the AMP the School had something that worked, something that had actually proved itself by practical results in the improvement of the men who had been sent to it for the three months' period. And the story continued that management was not going to stand by and see such a proven good thing wound up without registering the strongest possible protest.

Of course, as practical educators ourselves, some of us had thought we could see a number of good ways in which this kind of educational operation could be of genuine help in management development. We felt we had not been blind to its many contributions up to this time, even as a more or less specialized war activity. But the real spelling-out of beneficial results, whatever they might be found to be, had in our opinion to wait on definite word from the field where the chips were down in terms of day-to-day performance on the job. And it took the threat of abandonment to evoke the bill of particulars we thought it was necessary for us to have in our hand.

The details of the managerial protests dealt at some length with the inevitable imperfections of executive development left almost exclusively to chance. Of course, many of us who were close observers and participants could imagine what some of these shortcomings of the typical company situation were at this time, when the future of the AMP was in question. But over and over again they were pointed out to us, in the form of a complaint about how "narrow" this or that applicant's experience had been, or about how "highly specialized" it had been. And despite the familiar rotation procedure which was available to broaden a candidate's in-plant experience, they felt he "needed" the understanding of the other fellow's problems that both the course subjects and the multisided student body of the AMP had proved they could give him. If this sort of thing has been said to us once, it has been said a hundred times.

The frequently used example comes to mind of the research chemist who, outstanding in his specialty, had also demonstrated administrative gifts, or useful understandings about organization and about "getting things done through people," that just could not be allowed to go to waste. But his administrative talent did need formalizing, did need to be made more explicit and orderly and to receive cultivation in the right kind of reflective climate.

Another imperfection to which our attention has been repeatedly called is the hit-or-miss or "Topsy-like" character of the candidate's experience to date — perhaps better described as "lumpy," but in any event unusable and unadaptable owing to more or less protracted periods of aimless repetition of routines, to bad cases of malplacement in relation to an ineffective superior, and so on.

Along with this has been the complaint about the bad work habits that so easily accumulate over the years, and the resulting need for a general reprocessing or recultivation with respect to effective ways of facing up to a problem, of marshaling relevant facts, of considering alternatives, and of coming to a decision for action to be taken — all this to be possible in a challenging atmosphere of free debate, among associates bent on the selfsame ends.

Then also there has been the allied complaint that the man in question needs to be brought up to date in current thinking about good management, for which the AMP, in theory at least, is one of the obvious answers.

Again, one of the needs which has been hammered home to us, and which has always been of special interest to me, is the desirability of a complete break-away from the company-employer and its problems and policies, a chance for independent thinking about the company and the rules of the game that should govern its activities, an opportunity to live for a while in a wholly objective relation to the long-accustomed rigid patterns of thinking and acting to which the applicant has become almost slavishly subject over the years. "He needs to be shaken loose from old ways of thinking . . . to get away from imposed rigid patterns . . . a formal, clean break from his company for a while." These are direct quotes from letters we have received.

Broadly rooted in these same conditions, allegedly so typical of the company situation out of which the administrative chief finally emerges, is the need for some kind of dramatic handling of the developing executive's casual sense of organization, of his *very* casual appreciation of the enormous significance of the human equation in the solution of practical management problems.

Still again, the need has been pointed out to us of doing something about his blindness to the changing world, his staggering preoccupation with the commercial aims of his employer. This is a preoccupation that roots from the daily pounding away at the margin-making job vis-à-vis the immediate customer and almost entirely without regard to the general interests of the public — of the immediate community, the nation, and the fast-shrinking world. "This man has trouble seeing the woods for the trees," and "the School has been of great help to us in similar cases in the past" are the kinds of statement we hear more frequently than others might believe possible.

As a kind of sum-up of the whole argument of the need for this particular kind of developmental tool has been the charge that typically the emerging candidate for top-level management has unbelievably little sense of *administration* as a new and magnificent field of personal and professional achievement, viewed as a career quite apart from competence in the familiar great technical areas of functional specialization. And the educational need is manifestly for a fresh look, as provided in the program, at the whole content of the job of management. We must rigorously screen out the tasks of the specialists from the very big task of seeing to it that the specialists themselves are doing their work, both as individuals and in suitable combinations with others; and we must insist that this task cannot be left lightheartedly to heaven. (For some reason quite unknown to me the qualities and skills of leadership, which are really what I am talking about here, do not rate sufficiently high in the average mind to justify a respectable place in the hierarchy of available careers.)

Perhaps — as some have thought — we have in this AMP an inevitable extension of the formal schooling of the teens and early twenties — a schooling to be offered at appropriate intervals following the so-called "graduation" and following upon the achievement of major increments of experience with the concrete facts of life. What these "increments" of experience might be — two or three of them in a lifetime probably — would have to be searched out. But the point is that with each successive one the man should be ready to capitalize at a still higher level on his accomplishments to date, on gains made that only time and experience can give. Also these periods of schooling would undoubtedly serve as interludes of clarification and consolidation, of personal readjustment, reprocessing, and general repair.

I think two things should be understood and accepted about this kind of educational operation for the experienced man:

1. The purpose of such an enterprise should most emphatically *not* be further drilling in his field of specialization, except for the acquisition

and sharpening of skills in the use of the mind as a tool of analysis and decision, which would naturally be helpful in dealing with every management task. In fact the AMP "student" should not be *drilled* in *any* particular technical field, no matter what his personal history in his company might have been.

The proper educational job is to make sure that he sees the broad outlines of specialists' functions in running a business, with enough practice in trying to solve the problems involved to render his understanding of these functions realistic; but more than anything else to give him the opportunity to see and understand the impact of these problems and of the specialist's ways of doing things on people and the organization, on the specialist himself and on others who are affected by his decisions, and otherwise to appreciate the tasks of policy formulation, the framing of operating purposes, and the adoption of the proper attitudes to be taken toward the community at large.

2. The "student" should not be judged in terms of the skills or aptitudes of industry and studious application that seemed to come so readily when he was in college or high school. In these later educational activities he is simply doing a different kind of job as a student; he is facing different kinds of demands upon his powers. And I would submit that if as an advanced student (or as an older and increasingly experienced student) he cannot achieve entirely appropriate results in response to his classroom opportunities, then he is probably not fit to deal with the larger and larger tasks that his organization now has in mind for him. In the failure to comprehend this fact are the roots of some regrettable misunderstandings about this kind of "adult education," and in high places, too.

But to go on with my story — I have described some of the thoughts about the contributions of the AMP that began to be passed on to us in our little world when the end of the war saw us more or less lightheartedly accepting its demise. Of course they are by no means the whole list that could be drawn up. They are, however, perhaps amply illustrative of the ways in which this program by the close of the war was beginning to be found useful by businessmen not known for easygoing credulity in dealing with their newly felt need for "getting in the driver's seat" in handling the problems of executive development, or for leaving less of the job of building organizational effectiveness to heaven.

It should be added for the record that two of the companies that have done most, right from the start, to call attention to the "unique" benefits of the AMP and to make possible its preservation as an educational experiment are the Standard Oil Company of New Jersey, as immediately represented by Mr. George Corless of the executive development division of that great company, and the Norton Company, of which the spokesman has been Mr. Ralph Gow, executive vice-president.

Most of the needs of the developing executive I have been talking about up to this time, together with the hopes and expectations of employers about what the program can do to supply such needs, are, after all, limited to the things of the mind. In responding to these needs and to these hopes and expectations, the School has sought, with the aid of more or less standard tools of instruction, merely to do the obvious things — helping the student to improve his understandings of the job of management, helping him to better the quality of his workmanship as an executive and sharpen his natural skills or aptitudes, or — perhaps the best way to say it — taking *the man as he is* and adding to his command of the logics of the performance that will be expected of him.

All this is good stuff, of course, however obvious and typical of academic classroom operations. But more was needed and it was to be revealed quietly and only in the sequel of practical results as found in the man ready to go back to his job, or perhaps after some time of having been back on his job. These were the needs, and the work that had to be done on them, which were concerned with *the man himself*. Things needed to be done, it transpired, to add to or rebuild or rejuvenate his basic potential as a man, his basic motivations, his will-to-do; things needed to be done to free his spirit, to help him realize himself as an individual. And these things, in contrast with their more obvious intellectual counterpart above, are of course of the heart. Evidently, the School has contrived, somehow or other, to do something about satisfying them, too.

It would have been so easy, however, to lose sight completely of the nature and importance of this particular fruitage of the Advanced Management Program. Certainly our businessmen friends have said very little about it, very little, at any rate, that has been explicit enough to get hold of effectively. And we in the School have been so greatly preoccupied with the technical problems of running this kind of show successfully — the familiar problems of class size and frequency and of the nature and content and interrelationships of the course subjects — that I am sure that as "educators" we would never have had the faintest chance of uncovering any big hidden things of significance that might have been going on.

It has been our practice of working closely with the members of the AMP class, both in and out of the classroom, that apparently has opened our eyes — this and the fact that one member of the teaching Faculty, Dr. Charles Gragg, has insisted all along that not only were the big results being missed in all the appraisals that had been made to date, but that the whole aim of the course should be focused primarily upon the needs of the man himself rather than on the cold logics of the management job which has been so natural a preoccupation on our part. But regardless of how reliably I have interpreted Dr. Gragg's opinion of the proper conception and operation of the AMP, it has remained for the men themselves to make the dramatic separation of the big things from the little things, about which I am now trying to tell an understandable story.

Time and again I have had graduates of the AMP, or men close to the day of leaving for home, drop in at my office ostensibly to talk over or clear up some technical matter, only to have the conversation, before we realized it, get into questions about what the program had meant to the particular visitor. Almost typically the statement opens up, very casually and *always most unexpectedly,* something like this:

> Now I don't want you to misunderstand me; the courses have been fine, and all that. They have done a lot for me. But the big thing is what the whole experience has done for me *personally* [always with marked stress on this qualifying word].

And then, variously:

> I mean it has helped me to think through what I'm up to, especially to think about my company, how well it is doing its whole job, and to see more clearly what my own relations to my company are, and what my responsibilities to it are . . . It has helped me get a new hold upon myself. From now on I believe I'm taking off from a new and, I think, a higher level . . .

Or:

> I mean it has given me a relaxed attitude toward things; it has given me confidence — for the first time I'm beginning to present my own ideas about things or challenge the ideas of others and not just accept them as a matter of course . . . Things have begun to come out from under my skin that I didn't realize were there . . .

Again:

> I'm beginning to see that businessmen have professional responsibilities, that service to the community apart from the commercial sort has a top precedence, and I'm beginning to see myself as a member of a new and great profession, perhaps one encompassing all others, and new challenges of things to be done, and I'm getting fun out of it all . . . I think I'm beginning to see the importance of honest humility, and to gain a sense of my relations to others . . . I'm sure I'm going to be a better boss . . .

A very recent letter from a company tells us with apparent astonishment that the program seems to have *added to the capacity* of one of its promising young executives — "We don't know what could have happened, but clearly he has a higher ceiling than we had figured was his."

The AMP is a process, under all the monkey business and horseplay, of rededication of the personality to the tasks that personality is faced with.

What is it that lifts up a man's heart? What is it that makes him want to do better things, to participate in a coöperative endeavor? What are the things that unleash a man, that take the shackles off his faculties, off his powers? It seems to me it is our job to find out something about the secrets of whatever the things are that are doing this job of regeneration, and then ask ourselves as forthrightly as we can what kind of a job we do, trying to trace all this down and then trying to multiply the good things and to divide the bad.

Someone once suggested to me that an examination of the shackles which have been removed from executives attending the AMP might throw some light on the situation. This person expressed the opinion that the average college graduate is no more than a marionette in that from his kindergarten days he has been given assignments and direction so that he cannot think for himself, and this idea of initiative and thinking for oneself is intimately bound up with releasing these shackles and getting people to do things.

Perhaps, this man said, the Advanced Management Program is successful because the marionette who graduates from high school or from college gets a chance to meet reality in his business life, but it is still a guided reality. He still receives his assignments from his boss as he did in school, and this deshackling he gets in the AMP is actually his first exposure to freedom to think in the way he wants to and to pursue his own interests. This observer went on to point out that the best approach of all would be to have a man work for a number of years after graduation from school to get some practical approach and then, when he has been partially released of his bonds, come here and get what the students in our MBA program call the "Pot-Bellied Executive" treatment.

Someone also once pointed out to me that:

> When we think of executive action, we are obviously thinking of human reactions and human traits, and one of the most common traits or characteristics in humans is to tag people. Perhaps the chance that the executives get when they come to the Advanced Management Program is an opportunity to break away from the cataloging or tagging that the upper executives have placed on them.
>
> Now, in an organization we have various levels of management, and this kind of vision must exist on all levels. Naturally, we should assume that the best vision should be at the top and, therefore, the problem comes as to how to get it at the lower levels and, again, you can influence someone underneath you in proportion to the extent that the person believes that you believe in him. In other words, the big problem in all executive management is to get the top executive to the point where he can convince the people under him that he believes in them.
>
> If you don't do that — and I have seen management try to play down the lower level and say, "You are doing a lousy job," and not give a man proper credit — my observation is that top management has relinquished leadership. The leadership is then on the lower level because they have to have the stamina and the vision and the endurance to combat that depressive influence that comes down from the top.

I regret to say that we have been so busy since the war that we have not had much time to sit down seriously and examine matters like these. But pretty soon we must do it, or we are going to lose more face in dealing with this problem.

One final query: Isn't is possible that here is the real hunting ground, or research area, in which we can find out the best things to do in this job of taking the individual, adding to his happiness, and adding to his effectiveness as a member of the executive team?

Let there be no mistake about this: If the Advanced Management Program ever fails, or languishes for lack of spirited demand, the responsibility will lie right with the School, on the one hand, for a complacent disregard of the fundamental costs that have to be met; or, on the other hand (perhaps jointly), with the attending executive who defaults on his obligation to give the best of himself to the School and his associates while he is on this assignment. If there is a failure, it will certainly not be for lack of rich potential in the idea itself.

The Dean and the Faculty have very seriously urged other schools to undertake experiments of this sort — and I insist upon calling them experiments — from coast to coast, in England and on the Continent and in Canada, and are still ready to send members of the Faculty out to these various places to help them get organized.

Executive Compensation

By way of introduction to executive compensation, let us consider the very simple fact that one of management's jobs is the distribution of financial benefits from the enterprise. This distribution is a dynamic element in creating teamwork. We have, as was pointed out earlier in this chapter, the interest of the individual in belonging to a group. We also have the concern of the individual for advancement. And these two drives are rather difficult to balance, for the individual as well as for management.

In making compensation decisions four questions arise: (1) How much can the executive get? — a question of power and politics. (2) How much can the company afford? — a question of economics. (3) What is the right amount? — a question of morals. (4) What contributes to teamwork? — a question of morale.

Those are the questions we have to wrestle with in practice from day to day. My purpose is not to answer them but to bring them out for attention so that executives may clarify them by additional experience. I am choosing a problem of middle management and a problem of top-management payment so as to start our discussion at a more concrete level. It is tempting, but obviously impossible, to cover the whole of compensation devices from office space and parking privileges to profit sharing and retirement plans. Let us get down to cases with particular reference to the questions of morale and morals.

The first of these situations is that of middle management. One of the major problems in compensation is how to satisfy men who are making a career at lower than the top-management level, and how to encourage young executives with potential for growth.

I can illustrate the problem by a specific case:

Take a cost-analysis accountant, aged 37, who has been employed by a certain company for 18 years. His annual salary is $6,200, and he is married and has two children. The company feels, "This employee is one of the mainstays in our accounting procedures and manufacturing processes. As time goes along, he should be able to assume even more important duties in this phase of the business, but probably will never become a part of the top-management team."

An assistant sales manager in the same company is the same age as the other man, also married with two children. His annual salary is $21,000. In commenting on him the management says, "This employee is one in whom we have great hopes for the future." He has been with this particular company 2½ years, in contrast to 18. "In the brief time he has been with the company he has performed an excellent job in the marketing of two new products. He would have no difficulty obtaining a higher paid position in a competitor's sales organization."

That kind of situation, with people of the same age and amount of experience on quite different escalators, is repeated over and over again in countless companies, and in terms of management training its ramifications are far-reaching. At the moment I am not discussing the frequent differences between the compensation of accounting and sales executives. I want to emphasize another point: The first executive mentioned, with a salary of $6,200, will for 20 or 30 years to come probably be the boss for potential executives starting with the company to work in his department. Many, if not most of them, will be passing him on the escalator he is riding. In designing its compensation pattern, management must balance the advancement of a few stars with maintaining respect for the training positions of middle management, so a man will willingly devote his efforts to training those who are to go beyond him.

Another aspect of the same middle-management problem is the strain on those men who started out in their first positions at salaries beyond their capacity to produce because of lack of experience. They are on the $21,000-a-year escalator, and finding it too fast to keep up with.

The problems of middle management, these groups on the middle escalator from which promising executives must be drawn, are ones that require much more research. Here is a group of men who have little bargaining power; their numbers make the total dollar amount involved a significant question of what the company can afford; and at the same time acceptable administration of compensation is essential for a continuing sense of teamwork.

Our second illustration shifts to the level of top management. Here we come to the question of what the right amount is — a question of morals — in most large corporations, one of self-compensation. Take stock options, which have become a popular method of compensation since the Revenue Act of 1950. There is every probability that, given the right market conditions, the use of stock options will increase. They are usually applied to top-management positions, and so raise particularly this question of self-compensation.

With all the limitation and definition of the stock-option device by SEC regulations, the Internal Revenue Acts, and the Salary Stabilization Board, management still has important questions to decide. And most of these questions have a large residue of self-interest. For instance, who gets the options? Typically, companies have been restricting the number of executives who do so to no more than 25. Some companies go beyond this figure, but it is probably the most prevalent because it is the rule of thumb that the SEC uses in considering whether the securities need to be registered.

Outside the management group the questions are raised: Is the stock option for the benefit of top management alone? At whose expense do these executives receive it?

Then management must also decide how large the options are to be. Since the Revenue Act of 1950 made the tax treatment favorable, about half of the companies who have given stock options have been asking their stockholders to authorize between 2 per cent and 8 per per cent of outstanding stock, with 5 per cent the typical figure. That naturally leads to the next question: How often are options to be granted? In a surprisingly large number of these plans all of the authorized stock is allocated at once to the present members of the top-management group.

Other companies with more perspective have apportioned their total allocation, leaving to the board of directors the right to issue additional amounts from year to year. This assures potential executives that if they get into the top bracket, they also may become recipients without another appeal to stockholders.

The conditions imposed upon the exercise of options are another point of management decision involving executives' own benefits. Management must decide whether the options shall be exercised in two years, five years, ten years, or a longer time. Once an option is granted, the initiative (that is, the option for taking up the gain) is transferred to the individual executive. The most profitable time for him to exercise the option might be the time most prejudicial to the company's public relations, for example, during wage negotiations.

Payments for stock present another question of management philosophy in the matter of compensation. Should the executive accumulate the cash; or is the company going to lend money to the executive, have him pledge the stock, and credit dividends so that over a long period the executive will receive the stock fully paid for?

I have gone into the management decisions about stock options rather thoroughly because they illustrate the Achilles' heel of management. In the absence of united stockholder action, management is in the position of deciding its own compensation. Management must decide the moral question of what is right as well as the other questions of power, economics, and morale.

Just to illustrate the complexity of the problem, here is one more of the many questions that bear on the compensation mix and that must be taken into account: the growing issue of expense accounts. This is a direct outgrowth of the high level of personal taxation, for expense accounts presumably are nontaxable. (In some companies, for example, private automobiles and club memberships are taken care of as being necessary to the executive's business position.) Today, I am told, the executive who is going into a new job or new company asks, "What is my expense allowance?" as well as, "How much is my salary?" The proxy regulations that are being propounded by the SEC would make it obligatory to list the expense allowance for all executives over a certain bracket — one indication that the government is interested in the problem.

This raises again the question of self-compensation, or perhaps I should say self-policing, by management. If management is going to take a position of leadership, then executives are going to require self-discipline in not feathering their own nests, while at the same time insisting on fair reward for their contribution to the company. *That* is the fundamental issue.

Standards in a particular company largely grow out of the particular kind of teamwork which that executive organization is building. When we talk of teamwork, the pattern of payments for executives is the "pay-off." All the talk about morale and creating an atmosphere of coöperation in our organization is empty without adequate and just compensation. In the evolution of a dynamic executive organization, however, provision for executive compensation and executive development go hand in hand.

In summary, I would suggest that the compensation plan should reflect and reinforce the executive team at seven points: (1) in meeting new business conditions; (2) in attracting generations of young men with enterprise; (3) in giving dignity to the middle-management positions in which many executives live out their lives, coaching those who are to rise beyond them; (4) in focusing the energies of functional specialists and divisional men upon the job to be done, and not upon centralized or decentralized prestige; (5) in meriting acceptance of executive payments among organized labor, white-collar workers, and stockholders; (6) in gaining appreciation of the public and legislators for management of corporate enterprise as well as individual capital; and (7) in advancing the profession of management.

Conclusion

A great deal has been said in this chapter about the responsibility of management; about being interested in the other fellow; about taking into account what his feelings are, what his wishes are, what his welfare is.

On many occasions we have all heard a businessman or a professor or a public speaker expressing these sentiments: "We should do this for our workers. We should do this for the subordinates. We should do this for our employees. Make them happy. Pay them well. Give them pleasant working conditions." And then they too often bring in this last phrase: "If we do that, we will get more work out of them."

As far as I am concerned, that last thought spoils the spirit of the whole thing. It is probably a fact that more work will be accomplished, but let us view the matter in proper perspective.

I have urged my students and others, year after year, to believe that we shall be effective in the business community and more effective citizens of the world if we put into practice the best ideals we have, not because the cash register will ring a little louder, but because the people that are under our influence, whether they are our employees or not, know that we take a genuine interest in them as our fellow human beings.

I believe that leadership — effective, useful, acceptable leadership — can be best identified by asking: "Is this the kind of fellow that others like to follow?" If they *do* like to follow him, it is undoubtedly because they have concluded from their experience with him that he has the ability and the will — not just one *or* the other — but the ability *and* the will to do them some good and to help them develop themselves so they can do themselves some good.

THE ROLE OF MARKETING IN KEEPING THE ECONOMY DYNAMIC

Malcolm P. McNair, John Lintner, and Neil H. Borden

Let me open this chapter by pointing out why it is so vitally important, at the present time, that we keep our economy dynamic. In appraising our situation, we must allow, at the very least, for the possibility — in my own mind, the probability — that this cold war (or, better, undeclared war) that we are in is going at the moment strictly according to plan — that is, according to Joe's plan. We have been booby-trapped in the truce discussions in Korea with people who haven't the slightest intention of making peace in our sense of the word; and in the meantime, while that truce conference has been going on for more than a year, our mobilization effort has in many respects begun to fall apart. We have cut back our military program; we have postponed the date when we will be half-way prepared to meet any kind of onslaught, pushed it ahead from 1953 or 1954 to 1956 or 1957.

Washington's unwarranted fear of the probable impact on the country of the inflationary forces arising from the military program, in conjunction with political objectives in a presidental-election year, apparently produced this decision for a stretch-out of our military program. And then Congress wanted to go that one better, by putting a ceiling on actual expenditures for this current fiscal year!

This is not to deny that there is a great deal of waste and extravagance which is perpetrated in Washington; but the fact definitely is, as Mr. Baruch brought out so clearly in his testimony, that we are dangerously gambling with the security of this country by the program which we have adopted.

NOTE: Mr. McNair is Lincoln Filene Professor of Retailing, Mr. Lintner is Assistant Professor of Finance, and Mr. Borden is Professor of Advertising, Harvard Business School.

Mr. McNair contributes the opening and closing observations; Mr. Lintner sets forth the economic problems we face; and Mr. Borden discusses the role of marketing.

We have, for one thing, put too much of our resources into plant expansion and not enough into immediate weapons, and therefore it seems to me that the situation today, when we are trying to see what needs to be done and how to get people to do it, is a very precarious one.

I think that probably there are a great many complacent smiles of self-satisfaction behind the Iron Curtain, as the Communists begin to see what they think is the development of events according to prediction, in the economies of the Western World. In other words, they see us beginning to move into some sort of a depression cycle; they believe the long-expected capitalist crisis is showing signs of emerging, both in the United States and in Europe.

In many lines of business in the United States, particularly consumer goods, we are undergoing more or less of a cyclical recession. Meanwhile all the economies of Western Europe, especially that of England, are in a particularly precarious position, since their difficulties have been greatly aggravated by the burden of rearmament which has been placed upon them. We also can see today some of the same kind of world-wide tendencies in the overproduction of raw materials that we had in the late 1920's; while only a short time ago we were yelling about shortages, we now are possibly beginning to have the same overproduction of raw materials which precipitated the big depression of the 1930's.

It could well be from the point of view of the people behind the Iron Curtain that America is just beginning, now, to turn the pages of the last two chapters in the history of the United States as a free country. The next to the last chapter would be the one in which deepening crises, increasing labor strife, and social unrest would offer a very great foothold for boring from within, for fifth-column activities, and so on; and it might be a period in which both Japan and Germany would gradually be pulled out of the orbit of the Western Nations, with gradual intensification of subversive forces from within. Then the final chapter would be the one in which a quick, sharp blow at the industrial nerve centers of this country would finally "wrap it all up" for the Soviets.

I can readily see why behind the Iron Curtain they might think the nearby future is going to work out just that way.

What I am trying to stress, therefore, is that right now, at this vital juncture of our history, it is more imperative than ever before that we should maintain the dynamic health of the American economy. If we are unable to do so, we are going to pull down all the rest of the Western World into a period of very serious depression. We are so big, and our economy bulks so large in the total picture of the Western World, that serious business recession in this country could prove disastrous, could mean that the Soviets would be correct in their prediction of our inevitable downfall.

That is why it seems to me particularly important, at this time, to examine the economic problems which we face.

Economic Problems

Let us examine this Kremlin prediction and hope of the "big bust." Judging from at least a casual impression of the tenor of the remarks, a surprising number of American businessmen seem, in effect, to agree with the Russian prognosis. There is much of the same expectation of a serious downturn; in fact, quite a few businessmen, perhaps generalizing from conditions in their own particular firm or particular industry, even feel that the economy is already nearing what they speak of as the rocks. (There is, of course, a great difference in the views: the Soviets' expectations are based on hope, American businessmen's on fear.)

At the same time, in other quarters you find almost the exact opposite opinion. Many so-called experts in and out of Washington have pointed to the fact that when we taper off our military expenditures, we are only going to be cutting the federal budget by some $10 billion to $20 billion on the expenditure side; they contrast this prospective reduction with the $75 billion cut in federal expenditures that occurred between 1945 and 1946. Thus they claim that if the economy could take a $75 billion cut in 1945 and 1946 and still maintain high levels of employment, as it did, we certainly need not worry about a $10 billion or $20 billion decline in military outlays sometime in the next year or two.

Those who feel this way also point to the fact that civilian demands are high, and we still have ample sources of private credit to maintain those demands. They point to the tremendous amounts of investment that would be needed to build all of the new plants and equipment necessary to bring our industrial plants up to "modern" standards (by which they mean the best that we now have in existence). And they point to the continuous development of new products which will require new capital investment and also stimulate consumer demands.

Briefly, in my judgment, both outlooks are incorrect. I think that the bland optimists simply have their heads in the sand. At the same time, I think that the stark pessimists are ignoring many of the important facts of life.

As for gauging the $10–$20 billion cut in federal expenditures in prospect after we stabilize our military program against the $75 billion cut we had six years ago, the two situations simply are not comparable. In 1945–1946 we had been starved for durable goods, especially many important, high-value, large consumer items, such as automobiles and radios. That is not the case today. Automobiles are not backing up greatly, but cars certainly are not being sucked out of the dealers' showrooms; and electric appliance dealers are having no trouble maintaining adequate inventories — on the contrary, their worry is how to get enough volume to keep inventories in line. (The steel strike changed this situation only temporarily.) In short, we do not have backlog demands at the consumer level, such as we had with an accumulation of five years' near starvation for such items at the end of World War II.

Neither do we have the great six-year accumulation of liquid assets that we had then to finance these pent-up demands. Correspondingly, we do not have behind us six years of deferred maintenance, let alone the need to build up our plant and equipment to the measure of an economy that had virtually doubled during the previous decade. The Department of Commerce, not so very long ago, analyzed the new plant and equipment put into manufacturing since 1945 compared with the plant and equipment in existence in 1945. In manufacturing alone, nearly $50 billion worth of plant and equipment was added in the period extending to the end of 1951 — about as much as the gross book value of plant and equipment in 1945. Allowing for the price-level factor and for retirement, *new* plant and equipment installed since the war is equal to about half of our total current capacity. So we certainly do not have the tremendous backlogs of demand for plant capacity, any more than for consumer goods, that we had at the end of the last war.

We do have a real problem, particularly if we allow for the fact that gross private investment was running around mid-1952 at the extraordinarily high level of something like $60 billion a year. (I get this figure by pooling the expenditures of business on plant and equipment and including the housing figure, as is done in the government national income figures. The 1951 annual total was $59.1 billion, and I have simply rounded it off.) Part of this unprecedented level of outlay is connected with building the plant and equipment necessary to maintain our military potential. This program, together with much of the rest (devoted to civilian needs), is nearing completion.

Perhaps we will be able to maintain this level; but I should like to point out that a cut of only as much as 20 per cent or 25 per cent in the current rates of private capital formation would involve as big a cut as the anticipated magnitude of the reduction in our military outlays from the peak rates of some $60 billion down to the maintenance level of $45 billion or $50 billion now under contemplation. The reduction would be of comparable size, and may well come at about the same time. Adding them together, and allowing for the consequent reductions in consumer demand arising from such declines in income — that is, the cumulative effects — we clearly see that a substantial depression, in spite of the relatively small prospective cut in military expenditure, is very possible.

Nevertheless, as I have already said, this prediction does not put me in the company of the dire pessimists. I am not expecting anything approaching the serious decline we had in 1929 to 1932; in fact, I should be amazed at such a development. There have been many basic structural changes in the American economy since 1929 and 1932 which, whether one likes them or not, would be of great significance in the event of a downturn:

> We have insurance on bank deposits which removes the likelihood of a terrifying wave of panic similar to that which gripped the country two decades ago, both intensifying the severity of that depression and lengthening it over time. Also standards of bank supervision are better, and much of our mortgage debt today is under government guarantee. The fact that the potential magnitude of bank loss on mortgage loans at the present time is substantially lower than it was in the 1929 to 1932 period is an encouraging sign so far as avoiding a depression is concerned.
>
> Again, we have much stronger supports for agricultural prices, which along with the prices of raw materials are particularly variable; and probably also a greater rigidity of wages. Hence, prices of consumer goods, which generally move with manufacturing costs, are more likely to be stable. There are many exceptions, to be sure, in particular fields and areas, but this is the broad picture. In other words, here again is a stabilizing factor reducing the severity of the psychological waves, the cumulative forces, that carried us down so far before.
>
> In addition, there is the almost automatic increase in government expenditures which would mark a downturn, as well as the augmentation of private expendable incomes from unemployment insurance, social security benefits, and so on to offset the removal of people from the labor force.
>
> Also, I should not expect international complications to be permitted to depress our domestic economy as they have in the past.
>
> Finally, I think we have learned something from the experience and thinking of the last 20 years or so about positive actions that can be taken at least to blunt the force of a downturn.

Basically, then, for these and a variety of other reasons, I believe we have a much sounder economic structure, from the standpoint of preventing future depressions from approaching either the magnitude and catastrophic character of, say, the 1929–1932 calamity.

This is of the utmost importance in appraising our situation; but to avoid misunderstanding, let me emphasize that I am here concerned about resistance to serious depression. I do not mean that we are inflation-proof, or that there may not be a long-run upward trend in the price level, and I have not touched upon many other important matters. I only mean that certain basic changes — which are part of the factual picture and hence must be allowed for in our judgment as to how bad conditions would be if we experience a downturn — have raised the floor of our depressions. Let me also emphasize that this conclusion does not rule out the possibility of very serious depressions for individual firms, for individual industries, and for individual people. And I am not at all sure that the floor has been raised high enough to relieve the social and political tensions that a downturn would create. Indeed the possibility of serious economic distress is still present and is sufficiently real to require planning on the part of both business and government.

Private business can and should do far more than it has yet done to stabilize the economy. I urge all businessmen to examine their inventory policies, new plant and equipment expenditures, buying of materials, new-product development, introduction of new merchandising methods — in fact, all the areas of decision throughout the business organization — and to plan them with an eye to stabilizing their own operations and thereby avoiding depression. A great deal can be accomplished, and certainly as much of the job as possible should be done outside the government; indeed, one of the most promising ways to minimize the role of government in these matters is for private business to assume and discharge a greater part of the responsibility for the whole job of stabilization.

But that is not all. Suppose a downturn does start. That would be a most opportune time for business to turn some of the engineering talent now on the production line to investigating all of the possibilities for purchases of new equipment that cannot be examined when operations are at full blast. My impression is that tremendous opportunities for cost savings which could lead to profitable lower prices are always there for the finding, and that procedures for deciding when to replace equipment have lagged far behind what they might be, even in terms of what is now known. The tougher conditions are, the more need there is for improved equipment, such as will enable business to cut costs and still break even and at the same time help to hold up employment and thus consumer purchasing power. All these things, and many more, can be done. Some companies have already gone some way with this type of forward planning and action, but much, much more can be done.

I must leave the problem here: There is a tremendous job to be done, and the opportunities for private business to contribute toward stabilization have hardly been touched as yet. There have been some good ground-breaking studies of this problem, and some of the results have been carried over into the actual operation of business policy. That is all to the good. But there is need of more study and greater carry-over into business policy.

Marketing is one of the big areas where those contributions can be made, as the next section will show.

The Role of Marketing

We cannot have real stabilization unless the economy is dynamic; as with a gyroscope, the wheels have to keep turning at high speed or the whole machine falls down. And we cannot have a dynamic economy unless the people keep on buying things, more and more things all the time. Hence the importance of the role of marketing — a role that is often undervalued these days.

A development that has been bothering some of us on the Harvard Business School Faculty recently is the tendency of students not to go into the marketing field to the extent that they once did. I am convinced this is in large part the reflection of an attitude toward marketing that they have picked up in their undergraduate work — namely, that getting people to buy things, that is, being aggressive in marketing, is somehow antisocial and undesirable.

This unfavorable attitude toward businessmen's going out and influencing people to buy the new and improved products that are constantly coming into the market shows up more and more in the writings and observations of economists — and not only economists but other academicians. My children, who have attended three different colleges, have time and again quoted to me what their professors of English and philosophy have said about the undesirability of aggressive marketing, and particularly, advertising. Usually those utterances, on examination, have turned out to be not carefully thought-out statements but expressions of an emotionally antagonistic attitude — an increasingly pervasive attitude.

This attitude is completely at variance with the viewpoint toward marketing which has dominated our Western economy now for a century and a half — namely, that it is right to go out aggressively to seek business, to influence people to buy. The pragmatic view gives marketing a significant place in our scheme of things.

How can we account for the fact that over the last three centuries we have had a mounting economy, a progressive economy, a rising standard of living in the Western World, in direct contrast to the state of affairs in many other parts of the world? Large population and natural resources do not in themselves give a high standard of living. To answer this question of a rising standard we need to study the character of demand. We find that the answer rests largely in the social structure and the social forces that underlie our economy. Our society has developed customs and viewpoints that have favored a progressive, expanding economy.

With the coming of the industrial revolution there was a change in the position of the individual in society. Whereas up to that time he had been held closely by the traditions that were imposed by religion and by social attitudes, now, with industrialization, he began increasingly to throw off those shackles. In place of a static society we began in the Western World to get a mobile society. The viewpoint that the individual could better his position, if he had the ability and the initiative, began to develop. Any man could "ape his betters."

Kenneth E. Boulding, in "Religious Foundations of Economic Progress,"[1] describes the part that Protestantism has played in this development; he attributes a good deal of the new mobility of the individual, the breaking away from the shackles of static institutions, to the Protestant movement. He sets forth the "ethic" of capitalism, noting how "minor virtues" of thrift, hard work, and savings were recognized and became characteristic of our economy. At the same time he points out the weakness of capitalism: the

[1] *Harvard Business Review,* XXX, No. 3 (May–June 1952), p. 33.

fact that economic instability — the threat of a depression or the depression when it comes — tends to break down this ethic. For, he says, people lose faith in an ethic which is likely to destroy the security that frugality and saving promise to give. I think that he is right in pointing out that the greatest peril to our free market economy is the threat of depression; it is the one thing that the Communists are counting on most.

Then Boulding makes a remark that brings home this question of an adverse attitude toward marketing among academic people which was mentioned a few minutes ago. In commenting on the weakness of our market economy, he writes:

> The limited market leads to an undue shift of the emphasis away from production, to wasteful advertising and selling costs, to restrictions of output, to featherbedding and to other familiar devices by which individuals or segments of the economy seek to protect themselves from the impact of general deflations or seek to enhance their own particular power position at the expense of others.

Notice how he puts *wasteful* advertising and selling in the company of featherbedding, restrictions of output, and so on. Here an eminent economist in an interesting and illuminating article, in which he emphasizes the importance of the dynamic in our Western economy, makes a derogatory allusion to aggressive marketing, which is of the essence of a dynamic economy.

Now, there are many things about advertising and aggressive selling that may legitimately be criticized. We know that most of business's bad manners show up in advertising — sharp practices, dishonesty, and bad taste. There also is no doubt that advertising is often very wasteful, and that it sometimes has a monopolistic effect. Businessmen want to get freedom from price competition.

Dr. Boulding unfortunately makes this critical allusion to marketing and fails to bring out the positive, good side of aggressive marketing as well. In truth, influencing people to buy is a very important part of the whole economic process in the free market in which we operate. So let me reconstruct, just briefly, the role that marketing plays in a high-level and expanding economy.

First of all, we know that investment is the basis for a progressive economy. Unless we are constantly providing the means for increasing production — and we cannot do that without investment — we obviously will not have the increasing volume of goods to distribute to the people, as is required in an expanding economy.

It is basic, also, that investment rests on market demand. A promised return is essential to bring about investment. Market demand depends, in turn, on people's wanting things. The big question is: Do people just want more and more things of their own accord? Economists generally have by-passed the study of demand. They have assumed that production generates its own demand. But I think that every man who is in business realizes that demand comes from getting out and working to make sales, particularly, of those things that are not staples.

Now if you are going to get people to want things, the first prerequisite is a mobile society — one in which people are free to buy anything they want and are not shackled by tradition. We do not have to worry about that; we have had such a society for centuries.

The second prerequisite for a progressive economy is that people should have sufficient income to provide them with a feeling of certainty for the future. And that is where the depression danger comes in. The fear of depression creates an effect on demand that we have not yet learned to lick.

Now, in the long run, we know that if people have jobs, they have income. Jobs come from investment, and investment comes from the opportunity that arises when businessmen see a chance to make a profit. But none of these things happen automatically or without effort. Demand does not just come to the businessman who manufactures products.

Usually, innovations are slow to be adopted. There are "bugs" in new products that have to be worked out. Then, too, people cling to old habits and old traditions; and the larger the amount of money that is involved in a purchase, the more reluctance there is to be overcome. So, particularly with major new products, it is usually a matter of years before that important thing which we academically label "emulative consumption" enters, and demand really gets rolling and becomes important to the economy.

So much for really new products. For products that are established on the market, businessmen find it necessary always to stimulate people to buy them. To do so they constantly make innovations and improvements. Then they must work to get these improvements accepted. They have to go out and tell about their products. They have to convince the trade to take a chance on offering them; they have to try to make the consumers want to buy them. Thus advertising comes into the picture.

The error of the economists comes largely from the fact that even though they talk about the significance of a dynamic world as Boulding does very well in the article to which I have referred, they slip back into a static analysis when they turn their thoughts toward marketing. They are perhaps swayed by the prejudice which is aroused by the bad taste of some advertising and the evils of some high-pressure selling. They also tend to be preoccupied with aggressive marketing's monopolistic effects. In fact, it is inevitable that there be a certain degree of monopoly in innovations; there just would not be any innovations made in a free society if there were not a chance for the businessman to get a return on his investment. He wants at least a slight edge on competitors and seeks this through building brand preference.

Of course, the businessman strives to get an extra margin for his added quality or for his differentiation—just as long as he can. But, as anyone who studies the actual operations of the market realizes, for most products price competition sets in quickly, and the extra quality or the innovation is soon passed along to consumers without their having to pay a great premium for it. The public has benefited from the process, because improvements have come; investments have been made; production has been increased.

In the period ahead, it seems to me that we are facing a time when businessmen will have to be increasingly willing to take risks. A long period of good business tends to create flabbiness in our selling efforts; yet conditions are now such that there is a need for businessmen really to get down to work and become aggressive.

That does not mean, let me hasten to say, just doing more advertising. I think that there is nothing more pernicious than the idea that "we can lick the depression by advertising." The problem is bigger than that. The place to start is with the product and the price. The product must be such that consumers can be made to want it, with the price tag it carries. And remember that when business gets tough, costs do not make prices; the market does.

Then comes the job of getting out and working hard in the market, both with the consumers and the dealers, promoting aggressively and making people want to buy. I think the criterion of the size of promotional expenditures should be *as much as is needed to do the job as well as it can be done in terms of the results to be expected;* that is, each company should decide on its sales and advertising budget in terms of the specific tasks at hand. That, too, is the criterion for determining the size of advertising expenditure for the whole economy: if each company spends what it needs to spend in order to keep its own wheels turning at optimum speed, the total will be the best amount to keep the whole economy healthy.

If the economy is not kept healthy—if a depression develops and people become hesitant in their buying—then no amount of advertising just by itself will correct the situation. So I say here, again, that right now is the time for business to step in and do a better job of planning—particularly on its marketing—to try to prevent the vicious downward spiral from starting. If depression ever goes too far, our way of life will really be threatened. We must remain dynamic. We must keep moving ahead. To do so we must market aggressively.

The Challenge

The preceding two sections add up to a challenge. Let me conclude this chapter by trying to spell out that challenge a little more specifically.

I think that the best definition of marketing I ever heard is that of Paul Mazur: "Marketing is essentially the delivery of a standard of living." In other words, marketing and the standard of living are inextricably tied together. It is no accident that in this country where, on the whole, we pay the greatest attention to marketing, we also have the highest standard of living.

It is quite possible that one of the ultimate weaknesses of the Communist system will turn out to be the fact that nowhere in any of the Soviets' literature or thinking, so far as I can make out, is there any recognition of this dynamic function of marketing, this function of creating and delivering a standard of living.

We frequently talk as if marketing were something subsequent to production. But consider the great number of businesses which are the result of changes in the marketing processes, new types of distribution such as the chain store and the mail order company. Developments like this have created enormous opportunities for manufacturing that did not exist before. You can see it happening all over again in Mexico, with the introduction of Sears Roebuck stores there. Distribution itself tends to create the opportunity for manufacturing.

So I want to emphasize very strongly that marketing definitely does have a job — creating markets. In a sense, this is the reverse of the old mousetrap theory. It is the creation of a market for the better mousetrap that ensures a better one being made. Or, as the vice-president of the United States Steel Corporation remarked recently, "It is much better to own a market than it is to own a factory."

How, then, can we improve our marketing performance?

Such improvement is not just a matter of reducing distribution costs, which now account for about 50 per cent of the sales dollar. Actually, it might be that a combination of perhaps 75 per cent distribution cost and only 25 per cent manufacturing cost would do a better job for the consumer *if* the article reached the consumer, let us say, at a price of 90 cents instead of a dollar. The end results must be known before the proportions of costs spent on distribution and on manufacturing have any significance. I think that mass production and dynamic marketing *together* have contributed to a reduction of cost to consumers, and both can contribute more in the future.

But remember that distribution costs, in contrast to production costs, are not a matter of simple arithmetic. You know what you are doing when you reduce production costs; if you can reduce the manufacturing cost of an item 50 cents, and maintain the quality, quite clearly then there is no doubt in your mind but that you have done something for the consumer. But if you go out and slash 50 cents off the distribution costs, not knowing what you are doing, it may turn out that you have cut your own throat — and not done the consumer any favor either — because distribution includes so many interlocking functions and intangible services. In fact there are some situations where, perhaps, both you and your customers will be better off if you increase the cost of distribution, because then you may be able to operate on a larger scale and thus to cut prices to the consumer more than commensurately.

The basic fact remains, of course, that, while much has been accomplished, there is still much waste in all phases of business; and marketing is no exception on either count.

In improvement of marketing, integration of various distribution functions has already been effective — witness the big food chains with their long-run policy of reducing prices, and the petroleum companies which (allowing for taxes and changes in the value of the dollar over the years) deliver their products to us at substantially lower prices than they used to. Small independents can do the same thing by joining in voluntary coöperative organizations; this is already a strong movement, which is destined to go still further.

Again, productivity of personnel can be increased by better training, better methods, and by the use of machinery. I am convinced that the whole science of store fixtures can be radically improved; and that machines can be used to a much greater extent than now, not so much in actual selling as in merchandise handling and record keeping. Indeed I feel we are on the verge of a tremendous revolution in virtually automatic record keeping, on the basis of electronic methods already being utilized in some types of operations. (An interesting article on this subject is "Electronics in the Modern Office," by Ralph W. Fairbanks.[2])

[2] *Harvard Business Review,* XXX, No. 5 (September–October 1952), p. 83.

Much improvement is possible in the marketing of hard goods and the marketing of services, both categories in which the ratio of consumer spending may be expected to increase over the long run, or the standard of living continue to rise. I feel that our methods of distribution for hard goods, "big-ticket" items, still are lacking in effectiveness. Despite all the promotion by manufacturers, when it comes to the retail stage, these goods are "bought," not "sold." The marketing of services is something that we still know relatively little about; and as consumer expenditures for services increase, we need to study their marketing problems intensively.

In the retailing area we are only beginning to make progress in the effective combination of packaging, display, and use of store fixtures. Much remains to be done if we are going to make retail stores really efficient "machines" for selling.

Improvement in marketing also is related to the whole field of education — and I am not thinking just of the teaching of marketing, though some of us in teaching have been guilty of taking it too much for granted that everybody thinks marketing is vital and important. Somehow we must overcome the insidious effects of the economists' assumption that most marketing activities are superfluous, if not downright antisocial. The only way out is through education (formal and informal), through books like this, through meetings of businessmen, through professional organizations like the American Marketing Association — in short, by every means possible.

Education is important, also, in getting people to stop thinking in terms of the inevitability of depressions. At a conference of more than 160 business executives in the spring of 1952, I found that the group was strongly of the opinion that sometime soon — that year or the next year, or 1954 at the latest — we would face a serious business depression in this country. Well, if enough people feel and act that way, a depression *is* inevitable; and hence it is an important task for business and economic education to develop a broader understanding of the causes and possible controls of business fluctuation, and when I say "controls," I am not thinking so much about government control as about the things that private business management can do.

Finally — in line with the theme of "getting things done" — we must get people to recognize the vital character of this struggle we are in. Call it cold war or undeclared war or whatever you want to, it is the most serious war this country has ever been engaged in. So I strongly urge that more company executives, in setting their day-to-day policies, should take into account the kind of situation we are in; and, instead of looking wholly at the welfare of business, should consider the great public responsibility of operating their businesses in the manner best calculated to carry us through this crisis.

GETTING DOLLARS TO DO THINGS

Charles C. Abbott and Dan Throop Smith

Dynamics of Investment

Dollars, of course, do a good many things in the economy. They supply purchasing power; they provide the means for paying taxes; they furnish the wherewithal for investment; they are the root of rising production and an expanding economy. According to recent newspapers, they also furnish a certain amount of temptation to some of our weaker brethren in society. Most important to us, however, is the problem of how to get dollars to produce the kind of society that we want, and here it seems to me we must plainly put considerable emphasis on investment.

Dollars for investment come from credit expansion, from retained earnings, and from the sale of securities, securities sold either publicly or in private markets. Historically, of course, retained earnings have been the largest source of capital for business in this country, and I think they will continue to be for some considerable time in the future. Nevertheless, the sale of securities in the capital market, the continuous revaluation of existing securities, and their transfer from one holder to another are, in my opinion, essential elements in the free-enterprise capitalistic economy.

As a professor of finance I can go even further, perhaps, and say that a capital market is very nearly the core of a capitalistic system, and I can substantiate this view by the terminology which we commonly employ. It is, of course, a matter of observation that, barring

NOTE: Mr. Abbott is Converse Professor of Banking and Finance, and Mr. Smith is Professor of Finance, Harvard Business School. (Professor George E. Bates also took part in this panel, but because of transcription difficulties his observations could not be specifically included here.)

Mr. Abbott discusses the dynamics of investment, and Mr. Smith deals with the impact of taxation.

the Union of Socialistic Soviet Republics, no modern highly industrialized nation has ever developed without the concurrent development of a capital market. Holland, Great Britain, Germany, France, the United States — all have developed capital markets as their industries grew.

Notwithstanding this fact, there seems to have been very little study given to capital markets as such; we know very little concerning them. Here, of course, I am distinguishing capital markets from money markets and the extension of credit. There is an enormous amount of literature on credit expansion, on banking theory, on the theory of central banking, and so forth. But as far as my researches have gone, there has been no systematic treatment of capital markets.

Economists, when dealing with this general range of topics, typically talk in terms of savings and investment. Sometimes savings and investment are defined in such a way that one always equals the other; sometimes they are defined in such a way that a discrepancy can appear between them. I have no intention of getting into any argument regarding the difficulties of these somewhat elusive concepts. There is, however, general agreement among most economists and financial people that the ups and downs of investment are intimately connected with the ups and downs of employment, with the ebb and flow of business activity and the different phases of the business cycle.

It seems to be generally admitted also that when investment is large or getting larger, business is pretty good; and when investment is small or getting smaller, business is not as good as most people would like to see it. The point I wish to make here, however, is somewhat different.

I think most economists have usually dealt with savings and investment as if these were aggregates, as if savings or funds available for investment were homogeneous pools of money. In particular it seems to me there is a good deal of thinking and a good deal of writing which implicitly or explicitly takes the position that funds available for investment are all of the same general character, that they behave in about the same way, and that these different kinds of funds all have virtually identical aims and are, in fact, of the same type.

In my observation, nothing could be further from the truth. You have the funds available for investment accumulated by the small saver, you have the increments of assets that accrue in the large institutions, you have what one of my broker friends calls informed money and uninformed money. We all know that some of our friends, when they invest, are primarily seeking income, some are primarily seeking safety of principal, and others are primarily seeking capital gains.

I think it is a matter of observation that some kinds of money will buy equities and other kinds of money will not, and that there is a substantial portion of the funds available for investment that will take a position, let us say, only in triple-A bonds that are of the highest trustee caliber. In short, as I see it, the supply of investable funds is in actuality made up of many streams that come from different places. These funds have different objectives. And in the financial markets, indeed in the economy as a whole, they behave in very different ways.

While many of my economist friends speak of a deficiency or excess of investment in the aggregate as being an element causing business fluctuations, I should like to suggest also that among the different types of funds seeking investment, the proper balance necessary to achieve the goals desired for society may not exist, and, in particular, that excesses or deficiencies in the supply of particular kinds of money relative to the demand for these individual kinds of money are capable of producing serious economic maladjustments.

In other words, in studying the flow of investment and the action of capital markets we should not make the common kinds of mistakes that are made by some of the statisticians when they deal with aggregates and fail to look at the constituent elements of a series of figures. Let me give some examples:

It is generally alleged that during the late 1920's there was too great a demand — at least in the sense of the ultimate outcome of that period — for certain common stocks, especially common stocks of holding companies and investment trusts. There is a good deal of evidence, on the other hand, that during the 1930's there was a large volume of funds seeking investment in high-grade securities of a trustee quality, and that the demand was greater than the capital market or the economy could, or at least did, supply. At the same time there was a considerable shortage of funds willing to take an equity position or to invest in debt obligations of something less than prime quality.

Recently, of course, we have heard a good deal about the alleged shortage of funds willing to finance small business. Unless the political temper of the times changes, I suggest we may continue to hear more about this alleged shortage in the future. Other examples of a similar nature could, I think, be readily cited.

We also hear a great deal today about extending American investment abroad. If American investment is to be made in foreign countries, it is important that the foreign countries should encourage investment by their own nationals, and there are a good many countries to which we are contributing financial aid that do very little indeed to stimulate investment by their own nationals — or anyone else. I believe also that if American investment is to be encouraged in foreign countries, it should be up to these countries to make certain changes in their laws which would encourage dollar investment and which would make it easier for foreigners to own real property and to bring earnings home. Actually, there seems to be very little chance of this type of change being induced in certain foreign countries as long as dollar aid is available in such large quantities and is so easy to obtain. If I were in the position of these countries, I would not encourage investment by my own nationals, or by private Americans either, as long as I could get economic and military aid on virtually a "for free" basis.

At this point I believe another consideration enters the picture. Generally speaking, the kinds of securities that can be sold at any one time or over any one period seem to be those which the investors are willing to buy. The issuers of securities, the investment bankers, and the security houses can, in some measure, influence the taste of investors and affect the character of the market. It has sometimes been alleged that such limited ability as the investment banking fraternity has in this direction is an abuse. I have never quite been sure of the merits of that argument. In any event, it seems to me that by and large it is the investment demand that on the whole determines both the types of financing done during a period and the amount of particular kinds of financing consummated.

Thus, I reach this conclusion: The problem of investment, the problem of getting dollars to create the type of society that we want, gets down to the problem of so influencing the behavior of investors that they supply the kinds of funds and the proper amounts necessary to produce this desired type of society. This is fundamental. It is what investors want to do, and do do, with their dollars that largely determines the kind of economy we set up.

Let me tie this point in with my interest in dairying. I can put it this way: I think the problem is one not only of feeding the business cow the proper amount of dairy ration, but also of being sure it is a well-balanced dairy ration, with enough protein, mineral salts, fish meal, and so on to get maximum production within the limits of long-run efficiency. But this is a problem which we know a good deal less about in finance than we do in dairying. The record shows, I think, that we handle cows better than we do investors.

Impact of Taxes

Let me begin this section by emphasizing that people do things; money by itself does nothing. Thus, the problem of getting dollars to do things involves getting people to act.

Now, since people differ so greatly from each other as regards their objectives and motivations, any sweeping generalization about how "everyone" is affected by taxation is almost sure to be unsound. Yet, in spite of this fundamental proposition, one continually reads or hears very broad generalized statements concerning the effects of taxation. On the one hand is the view that, because of high taxation, our economic system is being slowed down to complete stagnation. Opposed to this is the view that taxation makes no particular difference, and that our financial and business system will, in one way or another, adapt itself to live with whatever form or level of taxation is imposed.

In our research activities here at the School during the past few years, we have been trying to work out some useful distinctions between different categories of people as regards the impact of high taxes. We have also attempted to analyze the relative importance of different specific features of the tax law. Since we seem to be faced with an indefinite continuation of very high total tax burdens, it is more useful to examine the consequences of particular features of the law than simply to bemoan the adverse effects of the generally high level.

When talking about the effects of taxation on what people do with their money, the first and most obvious point to note is that net income may be so reduced by high marginal tax rates that there is not sufficient return to justify the risk and trouble involved in business investments. It is frequently stated that high tax rates drive people from holding equities into tax-exempt investments. It is unquestionably true that many people have reacted to taxation in this way. These are primarily people whose objective is capital preservation and regular recurring income. For anyone subject to a 75 per cent marginal tax rate, 2 per cent on a tax-exempt security is as good as 8 per cent on taxable income — and where are the 8 per cent investments, anyway?

But there are also many other people who think in terms of capital appreciation and who, because of high taxation, are even more likely to invest for capital gains. There are an appreciable number of high-bracket people now seeking capital gains who would be content to hold taxable securities yielding 5 per cent or 6 per cent at a lower tax rate. We thus find high individual tax rates producing divergent and conflicting influences, depending on the temperament and objectives of individual investors. I shall not venture an opinion as to which of these two changes in investment policy — the shift toward tax-exempts and the shift toward capital gains — is the more important quantitatively. I am satisfied, however, that neither one is negligible.

Also, as the result of high taxation, many high-income people are being forced to place much greater reliance on retirement annuities and insurance than they would under a different tax structure with lower rates. Certainly for many executives the prospective income under their company's retirement plan bulks very large. This has significant effects on executive mobility and attitudes; it also constitutes another force leading to the institutionalizing of savings.

I shall at this point make some observations which I know will be highly provocative, at least for those of you who are in the insurance business. I am impressed by the many forces which tend to direct the flow of savings into institutional hands instead of leaving them for private control in individual hands. On balance I think it would be more desirable from a national economic standpoint to have the funds invested directly by individuals.

There is a feature of the tax law in this connection which I think will receive increasing attention in the next few years. As many readers may know, the net interest component in an insurance policy is in effect tax-exempt if the policy matures through death. This is not the case on an endowment policy or on any other form of policy which is cashed before death. From the standpoint of a high-bracket individual, the net interest rate at which these premiums are compounded is analogous to the interest on a tax-exempt security.

Many insurance agents I know are placing strong emphasis on this tax advantage of insurance in their sales activities. I am also well aware that the top officials in many head offices discourage sales campaigns of this sort, but they nonetheless are being continued effectively. I suspect that in another ten years, given a continuance of the present tax structure, this form of tax-free investment through life insurance will be recognized as somewhat comparable to the present use of tax-exempt securities in its perverse economic effects.

When I deplore the institutionalizing of savings, I do so with full appreciation of the fact that many insurance companies have taken the initiative in developing housing and other real estate projects, and that there are some significant moves in the direction of direct equity investments. On balance, however, the bulk of their funds does — and probably inevitably must — go into the legal-list type of investment, and the flow of funds in this direction does not seem to be one which needs to be artificially stimulated by taxation.

The very high estate taxes also have the effect of fostering a legal-list type of investment, by making it very costly not to leave property in trust for grandchildren or great-grandchildren and thereby avoid the estate tax on intervening generations. For a person with a substantial total estate, it is almost a matter of negligence not to make such an arrangement. With present tax rates and exemptions, the advantage of trusteeing property is very considerable, even though the total amount involved may be well less than a million dollars.

It has been proposed that there be included as part of an individual's estate the principal sum from which he receives the income during his lifetime. Many of my acquaintances who think I am a reactionary on most matters consider me extremely radical on this subject. I think there is a lot to be said for having the principal sum in which an individual has a life interest included in his estate on death. After all, when we are considering estates at the levels where taxation is a significant factor, the individual having a life interest in the income in effect has what for most people is the most important "incident of ownership" (to use the legal term). Both from an equity standpoint and an economic standpoint I believe it would be highly desirable to change the tax rules to avoid further encouragement to trusteeing and institutionalizing private investment.

What about small business? Has taxation been drying up the sources of funds and stultifying the growth of small business? Here again there are conflicting tax pressures. Let us look at the adverse ones first. The most common allegation is that a family business at the time of death of the principal owner has to be sold because of estate taxation. This is doubtless true in many situations, but it simply does not apply to the great majority of small businesses. After all, until the net worth of an individual approaches something like a million dollars, the total estate taxes are not likely to be enough to force liquidation. And the vast majority of small businesses are, of course, so small that an individual owner's net worth is much less than this sum. It is true, however, that in the range between something less than $1,000,000 and up to $5,000,000 of net worth the tax pressures for liquidation are likely to be strong. From the national standpoint this is, I think, an undesirable effect of taxation. In appraising the tendency to sell family businesses, however, adequate attention should be given to such other strong forces as problems of management succession and the desire for diversified investments.

From the standpoint of the growth of small business, high corporate taxation is especially serious because it reduces the amounts of earnings available for retention. In view of the great difficulty at all times, regardless of the tax system, of getting outside capital for the expansion of closely controlled companies, any reduction in earnings available for retention can be serious.

Those I think are the two main adverse factors. At the same time, there are some tax forces which are beneficial. In the first place, the possibility of capital gains in a successful closely controlled activity is probably much greater than in listed securities. Virtually all net earnings can be retained for growth and do not have to be "wasted" by being paid out in dividends subject to high individual taxation. This policy of retaining all earnings is in contrast to the situation in companies with listed securities where an appreciable part of total earnings must be paid out to satisfy the desires of small stockholders and from a general public relations standpoint. For those very high-bracket individuals who do not want taxable income, closely controlled ventures may be very attractive.

I am impressed by the fact that an appreciable number of such people are now interested in buying outright, or participating with others in buying, existing closely controlled companies or setting up new ones. A common procedure is to have the older generation take senior securities, with the children and grandchildren owning the common stock. In this way the entire increase in value arising from subsequent growth goes to the benefit of the younger generations and is not included in the taxable estates of the older groups. Thus we have tax advantages in closely controlled companies arising because of the greater possibility of retaining earnings which go to increase the value of a high leverage common stock held by younger generations.

If I wanted to stimulate risk-taking investment, I think I would look for a change in the treatment of capital loss rather than in any form of government guarantee or subsidy. If the $1,000 capital loss deduction against ordinary income were to be raised to $50,000 or $100,000, it would greatly modify the relative unattractiveness of new ventures for high-bracket investors. I would not propose such a change at the present time, because in the existing inflationary conditions we have in an aggregate sense all the capital investment that we need. When it is desirable to encourage more investment, however, I would strongly favor an increase in the capital loss allowance. The larger deduction might by statute be limited to small or closely controlled companies, if it were desired to encourage their development on economic or social grounds.

From what I have said it should be quite apparent that I believe the capital gains rate should not be increased. Much of the economic vitality which we now have in the flow of investment funds arises from the spread between the tax rates on capital gains and on ordinary income. The capital gains rate is important in an absolute as well as a relative sense, however. I do not know what the critical point may be, but I suspect that a tax which takes a third of a gain instead of a quarter might be significantly deterrent, and I am quite sure that a rate of 40 per cent or 45 per cent would be significantly repressive. From this standpoint I regretted the 1951 increase in the rate from 25 per cent to 26 per cent.

I am much less concerned about an increase in the holding period. In fact, I see little reason why the holding period might not be extended to twelve or eighteen months, or perhaps put on a sliding-scale basis somewhat similar to that which we had for a half year during the 1930's. I am well aware in making this remark that I am flying in the face of the opinions of those who emphasize the importance of a shorter holding period in order to encourage security trading and facilitate the distribution of new security issues. There is, I am sure, some merit to these arguments, but on balance I think the holding period is much less important than the rate applicable to fairly long-term investments for capital gains.

I shall not undertake to sum up these remarks or to express an opinion on where the balance lies among the various tax forces that I have indicated. My purpose has been simply to restate the inappropriateness of sweeping generalizations about the effects of taxation in getting dollars and people to do things and to suggest the sort of analysis which it seems to me is appropriate as a basis for an appraisal of the effects of taxation and for policy recommendations on tax changes.